VIEWS FROM THE SOUTH

THE EFFECTS OF GLOBALIZATION
AND THE WTO
ON THIRD WORLD COUNTRIES

EDITED BY SARAH ANDERSON

FOREWORD BY JERRY MANDER

AFTERWORD BY ANURADHA MITTAL

CO-PUBLISHED BY

FOOD FIRST BOOKS

AND

THE INTERNATIONAL FORUM

ON GLOBALIZATION

TEXT DESIGN BY DANIELA GOFF
COVER DESIGN BY COLORED HORSE STUDIOS

Library of Congress Cataloging-in-Publication Data

Views from the South : the effects of globalization and the WTO on Third World countries / edited by Sarah Anderson ; foreword by Jerry Mander ; afterword by Anuradha Mittal.

p. cm.

"Co-published with International Forum on Globalization."

Includes bibliographical references and index.

ISBN 0-935028-82-X

1. Developing countries—Foreign economic relations. 2. World Trade Organization—Developing countries. 3. Globalization—Economic aspects—Developing countries. 4. Globalization—Social aspects—Developing countries. 5. Globalization—Environmental aspects—Developing countries. 6. International trade. 7. International finance. I. Anderson, Sarah (Sarah Denny) II. International Forum on Globalization.

HF1413 . V53 2000

330.9172'4—dc21

00-058708

Food First Books are distributed by:

LPC Group
1436 West Randolph Street
Chicago, IL 60607
(800) 243-0138
www.coolbooks.com

Printed in Canada
10 9 8 7 6 5 4 3 2 1

CONTENTS

CONTENTS

CONTENTS

THE RESISTANCE TO
SOUTHERN PERSPECTIVES

Jerry Mander

President, International Forum on Globalization

IN FEBRUARY 1998, the International Forum on Globalization joined with Friends of the Earth, the Institute for Policy Studies and the Third World Network to produce a three-day forum in Washington, D.C., on the global financial crisis. The event presented discussions and recommendations on major changes that would be needed in global financial bureaucracies such as the International Monetary Fund, the World Bank, and the World Trade Organization in order to avoid such crises in the future, and to allow the values of equity and social and environmental sustainability to prevail.

Following that event, several of the participants appeared at a combined congressional and press briefing, during which Martin Khor, president of the Third World Network, summarized the southern viewpoint on global financial matters, and on globalization itself. Afterward, he privately expressed dismay at the general lack of knowledge in Congress about how these basic instruments (which Congress had voted on) actually operate, and particularly the way they are biased against southern countries in favor of global corporations. Oblivious to such biases, most attendees seemed to believe that these institutions were set up to help alleviate poverty within the Third World when exactly the opposite has been the result. Worse, they have helped reconstitute a new round of exploitation of southern resources and workers.

A year and a half later, in September 1999, in the runup to the WTO's Seattle Ministerial meetings, Mr. Michael Moore, director general of the WTO, gave a speech at the University of Washington in Seattle. During the question-and-answer period following the speech, Mr. Moore was asked why, given all the tremendous controversy surrounding the WTO, it continues to push toward a new Millennium Round of negotiations strongly favored by northern countries, particularly the United States and the European Union (EU) countries. Moore responded that, actually, it was not the northern countries that wanted the new round and an expanded WTO agenda; it was only that the North felt it would be helpful to the southern nations as they attempted to work their way out of poverty. In other words, the North was sacrificing itself to benefit its poor southern colleagues, as it had done in the Mexican and Asian financial crises of a few years ago.

Hearing this, I felt it worth reviewing the way that the United States and other northern countries, as well as financial and corporate leaders, tended to describe the Mexican and Asian financial crises during 1997- '98, and the way the media trumpeted those descriptions. According to those sources, the crises were rooted in a tradition of Third World incompetence, inefficiency, corruption, and cronyism. And the bailouts by the IMF—in the end by taxpayers—were made to seem like massively benificent acts of charity on our part toward these dysfunctional, underprivileged Asian and Mexican friends.

Rarely was it observed that the bailouts did not really go to these countries as much as to the American, European, and Japanese financial institutions that largely caused the problems in the first place by advocating and then stimulating overspecialization, overexpansion and export-oriented production within nontraditional economic areas. The net results were very bad loans, for the wrong purposes, to stimulate unsustainable financial bubbles that *burst*, bringing the bankers to panic. Taxpayers entered the breach to pay back bankers for their own horrible mistakes, but left the victimized countries in very rough waters. Banks were rescued, not countries. So much for free market ideology. What we actually have here is a system of free markets for taxpayers, workers, middle-class consumers and small businesses, but protectionism and cronyism for banks and corporations. Can't we call it cronyism, U.S. style, when a former banker, then-Treasury Secretary Robert Rubin, leads the charge to bail out his former banking colleagues? I think so.

Neither did the media explain the role of currency speculators in the Asian crisis. Under the new standards of global free trade and deregulation, there are few controls upon the massive movement of funds crossing national borders. With the technologies of global communication networks, currency speculators are able to move unimaginably huge amounts of money, instantaneously and invisibly, from one part of the globe to another by the mere touch of a key, destabilizing currencies and countries. This is something that many Third World countries are trying hard to prevent—Chile, Malaysia, China, and Russia notable among them—by means of techniques such as "speed bumps" that require foreign investors to leave their funds invested in these countries for a fixed period of time. This slows down the opportunities for the speculative investment-withdrawal-investment cycles that have often left Third World currencies and economies in disarray. It is only one of many efforts by those countries to resist financial domination by northern bankers and corporations; but most of these efforts are furiously targeted for destruction by proposals in the new

Millennium Round that Mr. Moore cynically says the Third World is seeking.

In fact, the WTO is seriously entertaining the revival of many aspects of the already discredited Multilateral Agreement on Investment (MAI), though these elements have now been carved up into smaller disguised pieces.

Reintroduction of any MAI-like rules could permanently enshrine the right of rich investors to dominate poor countries, which must retain some degree of control over the quantity and quality of investment on their soil if they are going to be able to encourage local businesses and workers and to build an economic base for the future.

Small countries are now still able to use a few kinds of tools—from tax breaks, to preference for government contracts, to requirements for a certain percentage of domestic ownership, et al.— that have given small farmers, local businesses and banks, and domestic industry a fighting chance to survive against the overpowering investment onslaught of global enterprise. Most of these tools were directly targeted for elimination by the MAI, and now also by proposed rules of the WTO.

How can Director General Moore still get away with the kind of obfuscating statement he made in Seattle in September, suggesting that the WTO, like the IMF, the World Bank, and the northern countries, are really dedicated to the welfare of the South? There are three reasons:

First, because the WTO has so successfully managed to obscure the reality of its own activities behind arcane language, utter secrecy, nontransparent procedures, and an antidemocratic structure. Second, because most in the mainstream media, until now, have shown disinterest and indifference toward the subject, and have easily accepted the handouts and viewpoints of corporate and government leaders as if they were gospel. Third, because his statements so nicely echo the prevailing paternalistic attitudes within the North that were previously reflected in the financial crises of a few years before.

◆ ◆ ◆

FOR A LONG WHILE, the International Forum on Globalization has considered it part of our mandate to try to expose this combination of unconsciousness and bias by various means, including teach-ins, publications, media work and the like, which help give some exposure to southern views. It has been an uphill struggle. Because the people of the South have been the most direct victims of globalization and also its most astute and ardent critics, it is crucial that their voices be heard.

This new publication is a collection of several views and comments by some of the leading voices of southern opposition to globalization and its expression within institutions like the WTO. It's our hope this will help break through a resistant western mindset on these matters and achieve some satisfactory outcome within the WTO itself and the entire global economic system.

In the pages that follow, the IFG is proud to present the pathbreaking analysis of seven leading southern scholar/activists. Four authors, Martin Khor (Malaysia), Walden Bello (Thailand), Vandana Shiva (India), and Dot Keet (South Africa) offer long, analytic articles that together will explain the complete history of the South's relationship with the WTO, and with globalization itself up to the present time. The articles also contain news of the on-the-ground effects among people and governments in the Third World, especially in the area of agricultural livelihoods, and exquisitely reveal the preposterousness of the notion that the South is somehow a beneficiary of this process. All four authors bring forth alternative agendas, slightly different from one another, either for a WTO that might theoretically be responsive to the needs of the South, or, *for no WTO at all.*

We also offer three shorter articles. The first two are by Sara Larrain (Chile) and Oronto Douglas (Nigeria). These pieces are edited versions of speeches that Larrain and Douglas gave at the 1998 IFG Corporate Committee's Conference on the Emergence of Corporate Governance. The talks focused on how corporations operate within their countries, strongly stimulated by neoliberal structures, and with what grave impacts.

We close with an afterword by Anuradha Mittal, an agriculture and human rights activist from India who now works in the United States for the Institute for Food and Development Policy (Food First). She comments on how some of the tragic effects of globalization are not confined to the South, but are also in "the South in the North," among the poor and working poor of the United States and other so-called developed countries.

ACKNOWLEDGMENTS

WE EXTEND VERY SPECIAL THANKS to Sarah Anderson, who took time from her crucial work with the Institute for Policy Studies to serve as general editor of this project. She did a magnificent and speedy job, and we are grateful to her for helping make this publication possible. Thanks also to Daniela Goff for design and production, and to John Cavanagh, Daphne Wysham, Debi Barker, and Katherine Wright for additional editing help.

HOW THE SOUTH
IS GETTING A
RAW DEAL AT THE WTO

Martin Khor

Malaysia-based Martin Khor is the director of the Third World Network, a large coalition of public interest groups and individuals with offices throughout the developing world. He is also a board member of the South Centre (an intergovernmental body of developing countries) and of the International Forum on Globalization. Khor is also honorary secretary of the Consumers' Association of Penang in Malaysia and was a former member of the UN Human Rights Commission's Expert Group on the Right to Development, and of the UN Secretary General's task force to review the UN system's environment-related activities.

In this article, Khor argues that the WTO system reinforces and exacerbates the vast inequities between North and South. At worst, the new trade agreements like WTO threaten poor nations' economic sovereignty, development prospects, environmental problems, and food security. Methodically, Khor describes the specific factors that conspire to keep developing countries in a disadvantaged position in WTO negotiations and dispute processes. He also strongly opposes the thrust of northern countries to expand WTO powers over new areas such as investment, competition, government procurement, and industrial tariffs. Finally, Khor concludes with an analysis, from a southern perspective, of efforts to link environmental and labor issues to trade agreements, raising questions about the effectiveness of this strategy.

M ANY CITIZEN GROUPS in the South, and many of their governments as well, are increasingly bitter and frustrated at how the interests of their countries and people have been marginalized and even stepped upon by the World Trade Organization (WTO).

Whatever hopes or illusions existed in 1995 at the completion of the General Agreement on Tariffs and Trade's (GATT) Uruguay Round negotiations—where the WTO was born—are fast fading in light of the performance of the WTO and the realities of its agreements.

The promises of benefits to developing countries have not been fulfilled. Instead, the obligations that these countries undertook in the many Uruguay Round agreements have turned out to be most onerous, and are likely to cause economic and social dislocation on a significant, even a massive, scale. National policies and laws are now being changed to conform to the WTO's rules, and more such changes are underway. These changes are going to be very painful, and for many developing countries there is going to be much more loss than benefit.

The officials of many developing countries were not really aware of what they had signed in the many complicated Uruguay Round agreements. The governments and people in these countries are now still trying to understand, digest, and come to terms with the many serious and structural changes they have to undergo.

Dealing with the serious problems of implementing of the WTO agreements will already be a massive task in the next few years as countries hurry to meet deadlines for compliance. Yet even before officials and citizens of the South can catch their breath, they are confronted with proposals emanating from governments of the North to inject more new issues into the WTO.

The earlier GATT system had mainly dealt only with liberalization of tariffs in industrial products. The Uruguay Round added several "new issues" (intellectual property rights, services, and investment measures) as well as agriculture to the system and transformed GATT from a contract among member states into a full-fledged organization, the WTO.

The developing countries were then generally against these new issues entering the trade system, as the agreements legally oblige them to change their national policies and laws so as to open up their economies further to foreign goods, services, and companies. Because their local firms and farms are generally small and lack the technology or marketing skills, they are unable to fairly compete with the big companies of the West and Japan.

There is a deep fear that when these existing agreements are implemented (after a grace period of five years for most of the agreements, which is now expiring), the developing countries will face many problems. Cheaper goods and services may swamp the market, replacing what is locally made. Bigger foreign firms with the latest technology or with marketing outreach will increasingly take more market share away from the local sector. This process is expected to cause retrenchment and dislocation, especially in the less developed of the Third World countries.

Even before these problems arising from the Uruguay Round have been fully understood (let alone dealt with), the big companies are once again pushing their governments to open up yet more areas for them to enter in the developing countries. In response to these corporate pressures, some major industrial countries are now proposing that another set of new issues enter the WTO through a new negotiating round. The issues include investment policy, government procurement, competition policy, industrial tariffs, trade facilitation, electronic commerce, and environmental and labor standards.

Many hundreds of citizen groups in the South are opposed to the proposed new issues, and to a new round altogether.

They think that there should be no new WTO agreements on these issues, as they would further restrict the ability of governments to regulate their economies or to plan for national economic and social development. The WTO would be intruding into the domain of domestic policy making in an array of critical areas. The economic sovereignty of developing countries would be greatly reduced and their independence would be deprived of substance. The colonial-era pattern of dominance of Third World territories by a few colonial master-countries would be fully reestablished.

The resistance to a new WTO round and the insistence that the WTO members urgently review and reform the existing rules and also the WTO's system of decision making are now top-priority activities of many Third World citizen groups and social movements. For them it is a battle to redress the inequalities and injustices of the WTO system; it is also akin to a new battle for national independence and people's sovereignty. They are urging and demanding that their governments protect their interests by resisting a new WTO round that would contain the proposed new issues.

What has caused this disillusionment among citizens of the South? Why are many governments of the South also sharing in this disillusionment? Why do they believe the WTO agreements and the WTO system itself are stacked against them? What are the massive problems of implementation (of the WTO agreements) that they face? Why do they believe a new round for reaching agreements on the new issues would be catastrophic for the South? These are large questions that require a full-length book to answer adequately. This paper seeks to give a glimpse of the answers.

THE WTO AS AN INSTRUMENT
TO GOVERN THE SOUTH

TRADE AGREEMENTS that are legally binding and have strong enforcement capability have become the most important vehicles for disseminating and implementing economic and social policies across the world, policies that have been planned by the few developed countries for developing countries to follow. The WTO, which is the main governing organization of the multilateral trading system, has in fact become the vehicle of choice of industrialized countries for organizing and enforcing global economic governance.

At the regional level, trade agreements are also proliferating. The North American Free Trade Agreement (NAFTA) is a prototype of a regional, legally binding agreement involving northern and southern countries, and its model may be extended to South America. The Asian Pacific Economic Cooperation (APEC) is another model with both northern and southern countries, but it is not ruled by a legally binding agreement.

However, the WTO is by far the most important institution for evolving and implementing trade agreements. The precursor of the WTO, the Uruguay Round of the GATT vastly expanded the scope of the multilateral trade system so that it no longer deals only with the conduct of trade at the border. Its scope expanded to cover trade and investment in services and, beyond trade issues, into intellectual property rights and investment measures.

The changeover from the old GATT to the new WTO with expanded powers and jurisdiction marked the passage of the age of trade agreements into a new phase: the globalization of policy making. The WTO is no longer only a "trade" organization. "Trade" in the context of the multilateral system has become a code word to include all issues that have come or may come under the purview of the WTO. Moreover, the WTO agreements have the most significant implications for noneconomic matters; for example, the WTO services agreement and the specific agreements on communications and information technology will have far-reaching effects on the cultures of countries around the world.

The vastly increased scope of trade agreements has tremendous significance—for the shaping of national economic and social policies, for the scope of development options, and for national sovereignty—and it creates concerns over equity and marginalization.

The conclusion of the Uruguay Round was heralded in the mainstream global media as a major triumph for the international economy and a boon for all countries. But at best the results are mixed for a minority of developing countries. For many others (especially the poorer countries), the round will have an overall negative effect that will further drain their economic resources. For all southern countries, the round will foreclose a wide range of development options.

Once a country's government has signed on to the agreements and enters the WTO, that country is obliged to follow the WTO's rules. As a result, domestic laws and policies in a wide range of areas need to be changed to make them compliant with these rules, even though this will severely restrict or constrain possible policy options in many areas. Noncompliance with the rules can result in complaints being brought against a country, and the threat of trade penalties and retaliation.

At the extreme, noncompliance can also lead to a country's expulsion from the WTO, and thus the loss of the automatic "most-favored-nation" status granted to a WTO member by all other members.

The WTO has thus produced a powerful system for ensuring compliance from member countries. Signing on to a WTO agreement is a very serious undertaking. In contrast, signing on to a UN Declaration, even a UN Declaration of more than one hundred heads of government, has little enforcement possibility and becomes only a moral commitment.

It would be very difficult, if not impossible, for a developing country member to change the WTO's rules, or to avoid compliance with obligations. What's more, the disciplines of the WTO are legally binding not only on present but also on future governments. Thus, it is not only difficult for a present government to retain any economic policies relating to trade, investment, sectoral policies in services and agriculture, or technology (vis-a-vis intellectual property rights) that are in violation of WTO rules, it's also difficult for future governments.

Should an opposition party have a different economic program, contradicting WTO rules, it would be nearly impossible to implement, whenever the party came to power. In this way, policy options have been significantly narrowed for the future as well as the present, for a country's policies would have to be made (or changed) only within the boundaries of what is permissible by the WTO's agreements.

INHERENT BIASES IN THE WTO SYSTEM: THE LACK OF TRANSPARENCY AND PARTICIPATION

THE WTO IS ONE of the most nontransparent of international organizations. Nongovernmental organizations (NGOs) worldwide have criticized the fact that they have little participation in the WTO's activities and that much of the negotiations are shrouded in secrecy. This is despite moves by the WTO Secretariat in recent years to increase the WTO's interaction with NGOs and the recent pronouncements by some WTO member states about the importance of involving NGOs in the WTO.

But an even more serious charge is that the WTO is even nontransparent and nonparticipatory for the majority of its own official member states, i.e., the developing countries. This deficiency is due to the working methods and the system of decision making of the WTO system as well as the lack of capacity of the developing countries to effectively participate.

Formal decisions are supposed to be made on the basis of "one country, one vote," or by "consensus," thus giving the WTO the appearance of being an organization in which decision making is democratic.

In practice, however, the GATT (the WTO's predecessor) and WTO have been dominated by a few major industrial countries. Often, these powerful countries negotiate and make decisions among themselves, and then embark on an exercise of winning over (sometimes through intense pressure) a select number of the more important or influential developing countries. Most WTO members may not be invited to these "informal meetings" and may not even know that these meetings are taking place, or what is happening there. When an agreement is reached among a relatively small group, the decisions are rather easy to pass through the various committees (such as the Agriculture Committee or the Trade-Related Intellectual Property Rights Council), or through the General Council in Geneva, which is composed of ambassadors of WTO member states.

The system of decision by consensus is also odd in its implementation. Even when a majority of developing countries (who form the vast overall majority of WTO membership) agree, the issue is killed if only a few developed countries disagree. The idea of "one country, one vote" is rarely realized.

By contrast, should the major powers (especially the United States, European Union [EU], and Japan) agree on a particular issue, while a sizable number of developing countries disagree and a larger number remain silent, the major powers are likely to embark on a process which they call "building a consensus." In reality, this means a process (sometimes prolonged) of wearing down the resistance of the outspoken developing countries until only a few, or even one or two, remain "outside the consensus." It is then relatively easy to pressure these few remaining countries to also agree, to "join the consensus."

The WTO has many committees and councils and there are often many meetings in a single day. Decisions and negotiations go on at these formal meetings. However, a significant part of the important bargaining and negotiation goes on in private, even within the committees and councils. Countries that are not considered significant are often not invited to these private negotiations.

There is also the major problem of the lack of capacity of most developing countries to effectively participate in the formal meetings of the WTO, which all member states are entitled to attend. Several developing countries do not even have a mission office in Geneva, due to a lack of resources. They thus do not have representatives attending the meetings. For many more developing countries that do have a Geneva office, it is usually understaffed. Typically, there is an ambassador and one to three assistants. They have to cover many duties, including participating in the many UN agencies in Geneva (such as the WHO, ILO, UNCTAD, Human Rights Commission) in addition to the WTO. Sometimes there are several meetings taking place at the same time in the WTO. It is physically as well as intellectually not possible for these understaffed offices to adequately monitor all the developments in the WTO, let alone be able to formulate well-informed negotiation positions. Moreover, the Geneva-based officials are required to refer important decisions to their ministries in the capital. And at the capital, there is also a lack of capacity to monitor and respond to the requests of the Geneva office, as the unit dealing with WTO issues may have only one or two people.

This lack of capacity of developing countries is in stark contrast to the huge negotiating machinery of developed countries, which have many staffmembers at both at the negotiating arenas and in the ministries at the capital, backed up by researchers, academics, and research institutions. They are able not only to formulate precise language and positions in the negotiations on many issues (taking into account the substantive and the legal aspects) but also to design a framework of long-term trade strategies, and then plan negotiating strategies and positions around them.

On the other hand, developing countries are swamped by the challenge of implementing existing agreements in ways least damaging to their economies and are hardly able to keep track of the flood of new proposals and positions coming from the developed countries (and from other developing countries). Individually, they cannot adequately respond to these new proposals and positions, nor can they collaborate with other developing countries to develop common positions.

Developing countries are simply no match for the gigantic planning and negotiating machinery of the North. There is thus a gross inequity in the WTO, because negotiations and the formulation of rules (and the defense of a country's compliance or noncompliance with its obligations) is at the center of the WTO's activities. Given the gross imbalance in bargaining and negotiating capacities between North and South (as well as the manipulative devices that the major industrial countries have mastered), the rich nations normally had their way in GATT and now have it in the WTO. Issues that they do not want to enter the system, or to be highlighted, are not allowed to emerge in the WTO. By contrast, issues that the northern countries agree upon are given prominence and are pushed, even against the wishes of many developing countries, until new agreements are reached. In the negotiations, the interpretation of the powerful countries on how an issue should be treated is very likely to prevail, due to their much stronger negotiating capacity and bargaining position.

Recently, in the selection of the new director general of WTO, there was a lack of transparency in the entire process. One of the candidates (Supachai Panitchpakdi of Thailand) was in the lead by a significant margin for much of the period, but there was no attempt by the General Council chairman to "form a consensus" around him. The United States campaigned strongly for the other candidate (Michael Moore of New Zealand). When support was mustered, so that it was claimed he had one or two more supporters than Supachai, the chairman of the WTO Council announced that a consensus should be formed around Moore. Many developing countries among Supachai's supporters (there were also some developed countries supporting him) cried foul, decried the nontransparent process, and demanded that a vote be taken. The United States and other developed countries did not want a vote because this would set a precedent (there has never been a vote taken in the WTO) and damage the "decision by consensus" system. In the end, a compromise was reached, with Moore taking a three-year term, to be followed by a three-year term for Supachai. The whole process, which lasted several months, was most bitter, unsatisfactory, and nontransparent. A more transparent approach would have been to take a vote at a predetermined date.

In 1996, developed countries lobbied very hard to have three topics (investment, competition, and government procurement) introduced as new issues for study and eventual negotiation for agreements in the WTO. They wanted the Ministerial Conference in Singapore in December 1996 to endorse this. During the preparatory process, a significant number of developing countries vocally objected. Thus, there was clearly no consensus. Nevertheless, the issues became the main topic at the Ministerial. The director general wrote a letter to the chairman of the Ministerial requesting the latter to consider taking up the three issues on which there was no consensus, and to establish a small "informal group" of thirty countries to negotiate the final text of the Ministerial Declaration. Who selected the thirty countries, and on what basis—and what it was they were discussing—were not known to the conference delegates as a whole. Only on the night before the conference ended were all the delegations summoned, given the final draft that had been thrashed out in secret by the small group, and asked to endorse it without change. Although several of the ministers protested the nontransparent and undemocratic process, the draft was eventually adopted unchanged as the Ministerial Declaration. In it were the decisions to establish the three new working groups, on investment, competition, and government procurement, that had only a few days earlier been objected to by many developing countries.

The lack of transparency is so serious that many of the representatives of the member states are not given adequate information and are not able to participate meaningfully. Further, manipulative devices are used to ensure that the decisions desired by the few members that dominate the system are achieved, while the policies or decisions that many or most developing countries want are ignored or deflected and have little or no chance of success.

The above features of the WTO system explain why developing countries are at such an immense disadvantage, and why it is so likely that issues brought into or discussed at the WTO are skewed and biased toward the interests of the major developed countries, whose governments effectively represent their commercial and corporate interests.

INEQUITIES BETWEEN NORTH AND SOUTH
IN THE WTO AGREEMENTS

A. THIRD WORLD SCHOLARS CRITIQUE THE URUGUAY ROUND
THE URUGUAY ROUND negotiations that gave birth to the WTO resulted in a package of agreements that were, on the whole, unbalanced and inequitable in favor of developed countries. Various aspects of the asymmetries and disadvantages to developing countries have been brought out in several studies (for example, Raghavan 1990, 1995; Das 1996, 1997; South Centre 1995; Dubey 1995; Nayyar 1995; G. Corea 1995; Shahin 1996).

According to Raghavan (1995): "From the perspective of developing countries generally (and more so of their poor and disadvantaged sections), the new trade order under the WTO has more negative than positive features. And while it could be beneficial as a rule-based system (depending on how the major industrialized countries implement it in letter and spirit), the rules in some areas of obligations for the majors are ambiguous and vague, while those relating to developing countries are specific and quite onerous such as in Trade Related Intellectual Property Rights (TRIPs), where the original purpose of intellectual property rights (namely, rewarding innovation while ensuring disclosure and sharing of knowledge for enabling further innovation), has now been overtaken by attempts to cater to the greed of the corporations and to safeguard their investments."

Studies by Bhagirath Lal Das (1997, 1998) conclude that the Uruguay Round "has been a unique negotiation in which most of the concessions have been made by developing countries without getting anything but meager concessions in return. It is not because the negotiators or trade policy officials of developing countries ignored the interests of their countries...The results are in fact characterized by the massive gap between the economic and political strengths of developed and developing countries." In a more comprehensive study, Das (1998) analyzes the severe overall imbalance in concessions made by South and North and how the recent trend in the WTO enhances the imbalance. It then examines the imbalances and deficiencies in various areas: the dispute settlement system; market access; balance of payments and safeguards; subsidies and dumping; specific sectors like agriculture and textiles; the new issues of services and intellectual property rights (IPRs); neo-protectionism; and commitments of developed countries.

Referring to the WTO agreements, the Indian economics professor Deepak Nayyar (1995) states: "It would seem that the institutional framework for globalization is characterized by a striking asymmetry. National boundaries should not matter for trade flows and capital flows but should be clearly demarcated for technology flows and labor flows. It follows that the developing countries would provide access to their markets without a corresponding access to technology and would accept capital mobility without a corresponding provision for labor mobility. This asymmetry, particularly that between the free movement of capital and the 'unfree' movement of labor across national boundaries, lies at the heart of the inequality in the rules of the game for globalization in the late twentieth century. These new rules, which serve the interests of transnational corporations in the process of globalization, are explicit as an integral part of a multilateral regime of discipline."

A significant critique of the outcome of the Uruguay Round was also made in 1994 by Luis Fernando Jaramillo, then chairman of the Group of 77 in New York and Colombia's permanent representative to the United Nations. In a speech after the round's conclusion, he stated: "The Uruguay Round is proof again that the developing world continues to be sidelined and rejected when it comes to defining areas of vital importance for their survival. The Third World confined itself to a role of passive spectator of the decisions adopted…The countries of the Third World have been put in a situation in which they already paid the price of accepting the new terms in different areas of interest for the industrialized countries, without obtaining in exchange satisfactory conditions of market access…According to some estimates, the industrialized countries, which make up only 20 percent of the GATT membership, will appropriate 70 percent of the additional income that will be generated by the implementation of the Uruguay Round. It would seem that this does not allow one to conclude that the Uruguay Round will translate into a positive balance to developing countries…Unquestionably, the developing countries are the losers both individually and collectively."

B. THE URUGUAY ROUND'S COMBINATION OF LIBERALIZATION AND PROTECTIONISM FOR CORPORATE INTERESTS

IT IS A MISTAKEN NOTION that the Uruguay Round was set up to promote liberalization overall. As pointed out by Nayyar, the main asymmetry in the round's results was that the northern countries obtained liberalization in areas where it would benefit them and protectionism in areas where it would not (i.e., technology and IPRs). Moreover, the proposal by some developing countries for liberalization of labor services was unacceptable to the North.

When the round began in 1986, many Third World countries were strongly resisting the northern countries' push to expand GATT's powers into "new areas" such as services, investments, and IPRs. Up to then, GATT's jurisdiction was only over the rules of trade in manufactured goods. The southern countries were rightly concerned that the North was interested in liberalizing economic areas in which they had an advantage: where their corporations could penetrate and capture new markets that until then had been relatively protected by southern governments.

This was certainly the case in services, a rapidly expanding sector, with transnational enterprises including banks, insurance companies, and movie studios eagerly awaiting the removal of barriers to their advance into Third World markets.

The negotiations over trade-related investment measures (TRIMs) were similarly initiated by the North to pressure Third World governments to give up their powers to impose conditions on the entry and operations of foreign companies. The "liberalization" of investments would clearly benefit the North, where most transnational companies are based. The South was concerned that with only weak restrictions permitted to be placed on these big corporations, the smaller-scale domestic businesses would not survive the onslaught of foreign investments.

On the other hand, when it came to the subject of technology transfer, the North took an aggressively antiliberalization stance and instead pushed for compulsory introduction of a standard set of national laws to protect intellectual property rights. Since most patents are owned by transnational companies, in effect this meant the legal protection of technological monopoly by these northern-owned firms and a drastic curtailment of possibilities by the South to learn and use new technologies.

The North's motives for introducing trade-related intellectual property rights (TRIPs) in the round were:

◆ to enable their firms to capture more profits through monopolistic higher prices and through royalties and the sale of technology products and

◆ to put in place stiff barriers preventing the technological development of potential new rivals from the South.

The northern countries' push in TRIPs proved that "free trade" and "liberalization" were only nice slogans to move the round forward. The reality was that they would promote their own commercial interests, whether that meant through liberalization or protectionism.

In the early and middle stages of the round, several Third World countries (including influential countries like India and Brazil) put up stiff resistance to the northern push and interpretation of the "new areas." But by the final two years, the southern fight had melted, and in the end the round adopted rules to protect IPRs, liberalize services, and prohibit trade-related investment measures. All three issues have thus become integrated with trade in manufactured and agricultural goods, and all now fall under the jurisdiction of the WTO.

In effect, the Uruguay Round has most benefited the transnational corporations. The free trade so much bandied about by the proponents of the round has come to mean, in reality, the vastly expanded freedom and powers of transnational corporations to trade and invest in most countries of the world. Correspondingly, governments now have significantly reduced powers to restrict corporate "freedom" from potential new competitors whose possibilities to develop technologically are now curbed by intellectual property provisions in TRIPs. The big companies, which propelled the northern governments from start to end, have won many more rights without having to meet new obligations. Indeed, previous obligations they may have had to observe are now dropped.

DIFFICULTIES FOR DEVELOPING COUNTRIES GENERATED BY THE WTO AGREEMENTS AND THEIR PROBLEMS OF IMPLEMENTATION

ON THE WHOLE, the conclusion of the Uruguay Round and the formation of the WTO has benefited the rich industrial nations. Most developing countries (especially the least developed and weaker economies) have lost out. They have been unable to take advantage of any additional potential export opportunity, because they are also obliged to open up more deeply and in more sectors, threatening the survival of their local firms and farms.

The Uruguay Round was expected to bring some benefits to those developing countries able to take advantage of certain changes, but even those benefits have not been significant thus far. The following are some examples of potential benefits that have not materialized:

- A lowering of northern countries' industrial tariffs may benefit those southern countries with a manufacturing export capacity. Even then, the reduction of average industrial tariffs in developed countries has only been from 6.3 percent to 3.8 percent, which means that an imported product costing $100 before duty could enter after duty at $104 instead of the previous $106, which is not a significant reduction. And "tariff peaks" (or higher-than-average import duties) remain for many products that developing countries export. For instance the U.S. tariff for orange juice is 31 percent.

- The phase-out of the multifiber arrangement (which has allowed northern countries to place quotas on imports of textiles, clothing, and footwear) was supposed to be the aspect of the Uruguay Round to most immediately benefit the South, or at least the countries that export these products. So far, however, these countries have not seen tangible benefits. This is because developed countries "end-loaded" their implementation schedules so that most of the products they buy from developing countries will only be liberalized at the end of the ten-year phase-out period. There is also a fear that nontariff barriers will be used to continue to block Third World products when the phase-out of tariffs is completed.

- The Agreement on Agriculture (AOA) was supposed to result in the reduction of agricultural subsidies in the North, and this was expected to improve the market access of those southern countries that export agricultural products. As it turned out, however, the agreement allowed the developed countries to maintain most of the high subsidies that existed prior to the conclusion of the Uruguay Round. For example, they are obliged to reduce domestic subsidies by only 20 percent. In contrast, most developing countries had no or little domestic or export subsidies. They are now barred by the AOA from having them or raising them in the future.

- The weaker developing countries, without much export capacity, were not expected to benefit much at all from the Uruguay Round. Several countries (especially in Africa, but also including Indonesia) were projected to suffer absolute losses from the agreements. The benefits (which fall significantly short of what had been requested by the developing countries) were also projected to take a long time (ten to twenty years) to come on stream, while the problems of compliance are already being felt by developing countries.

In exchange for some uneven and very limited benefits in the Uruguay Round, the South as a whole has had to make major concessions, especially in agreeing to bring in the new issues of services, investment measures, and intellectual property rights. Even for agriculture, many developing countries are in danger of having their food security and farmers' livelihoods come under threat, as explained below.

Thus, another set of problems striking at developing countries are those they face when they change their economic policies at the national level to comply with their WTO obligations. Examples of these problems are as follows:

Agreement on Agriculture (AOA)
The AOA could have severe negative effects on many Third World countries. Most of them (except the least developed countries) will have to reduce domestic subsidies to farmers and remove nontariff controls on agricultural products, convert these

to tariffs, and then progressively reduce them. This will impose global competition on the domestic farm sector. Farmers unable to compete with cheaper imports may not survive. Hundreds of millions of small Third World farmers could be affected. Agricultural liberalization will also raise world food prices, which may benefit food exporters but about one hundred Third World food importing countries will face a higher food import bill.

Services

The Uruguay Round brought services into the GATT system for the first time. Although at this stage blanket liberalization is not required, developing countries will experience far more pressure to liberalize their services sectors. Currently, many Third World countries provide some protection for the services sector, allowing the development of local enterprises in banking, insurance, trade, the media, and professional services. It is feared that under the pressures of liberalization, the northern corporations involved in services will make further inroads and in some countries may come to dominate some of the services.

The Agreement on Trade-Related Intellectual Property Rights (TRIPs)

The South's collective loss was most acutely felt in the agreement on trade-related intellectual property rights (TRIPs), through which countries are obliged to introduce IPR legislation with standards of protection that are similar to those of northern countries. This will hinder the southern countries' indigenous technological development. It should be noted that the present industrial countries did not have patent or IPR laws, or laws as strict as will now be imposed through TRIPs, during their industrializing period, and this enabled them to incorporate technology design originating from abroad into their local systems.

TRIPs will also give rise to increasing technical payments such as royalties and license fees to corporations owning most of the world's patents.

The new IPR regime will also have significant impact on raising the prices of many products. By restricting competition, the IPR rules will enable some companies to jack up the prices of their products far beyond costs and thus earn rents in terms of monopoly revenues and profits. This is clearly seen in the case of computer software.

Also, most Third World countries have in the past exempted agriculture, medicines, and other essential products and processes from their national patent laws. But with the passage of TRIPs everything is subject to IPR law, unless explicitly exempted. The prices of medicines are expected to shoot up in many countries, and foreign drug sales will increase rapidly at the expense of local products.

The TRIPs agreement also opens the door to the patenting of life forms such as microorganisms and modified genetic materials, thus providing the boost in incentives so much desired by the biotechnology industry. Many environmentalists are concerned that this will be detrimental to the global environment because the present lack of controls and accountability in biotechnology research and application will likely accelerate biodiversity loss and could threaten natural ecosystems.

For plant varieties, TRIPs does permit countries the option to either introduce patents or an alternative "effective" sui generis (unique) system of intellectual property protection for a trial period of four years, after which the agreement will be reviewed. Many farmers' groups (especially in India, where huge farmers' demonstrations and rallies have been held against the WTO) and environmentalists are concerned that, in the end, Third World farmers will not be allowed to follow the traditional practice of saving seed for the next season's planting. If the seed is under a company's IPR protection, it could ban this practice, forcing farmers to purchase seed yearly.

Trade-Related Investment Measures (TRIMs)

In the area of TRIMs, the most important point is that national policies relating to foreign investments have also now explicitly come under the ambit of the GATT/WTO system. Originally, the northern countries proposed an agreement on investment policy per se, in which foreign companies were to be given an automatic "right to establishment" or "commercial presence." This would have given rights to foreign companies with the stroke of a pen that were attained by the colonizers through war and bloodshed. Eventually, the objections of some developing countries prevailed.

In the final TRIMs agreement, "investment measures" such as local content (obliging foreign firms to use a specified minimal amount of local inputs) will be phased out. This of course has serious enough implications in terms of prohibiting measures that promote local industry and greater linkages to the domestic economy and that protect the balance of payments. In implementing TRIMs, developing countries will lose some important policy options to pursue their industrialization.

Just as significantly, the explicit introduction of investment issues into the WTO opened the door for the northern governments to resume their efforts to bring in the whole body of "investment policy per se." And, in fact, there is now intense pressure from the North to establish an investment agreement in the WTO along the lines of the failed Multilateral Agreement on Investment (MAI) model in the Organization for Economic Cooperation and Development (OECD).

THE NEED TO REVIEW AND REPAIR
THE WTO AGREEMENTS

GIVEN THE SERIOUS CHALLENGES faced by developing countries in implementing their Uruguay Round commitments (and in dealing with improper implementation by the developed countries), there should be a review of many of the agreements with a view to amending them. In fact, many of the agreements themselves mandate that reviews be carried out four or five years after coming into force.

The next three to five years of the WTO's activities should focus on the review process, to provide an opportunity to rectify the defects of the agreements. This review process would in itself be a massive task, involving analyses of the weaknesses of the various agreements, assessments of how they have affected or will affect developing countries, proposals to amend the agreements, and negotiations on these proposals.

A good indication of the enormity of the task is provided by the recent writings of Bhagirath Lal Das (1998, 1999), who has compiled an analysis of the deficiencies and imbalances of many of the agreements and provided suggestions on how they can be rectified.

A few examples of the need to amend some agreements, and of the way this could be done, are as follows:

TRIPs Agreement Article 27.3(b)

This article deals with the patenting of life forms and the intellectual property protection of plant varieties, issues that are of major concern to developing countries, to farmers' groups, environmental groups, and civil society worldwide. A review of this article is mandated to begin in 1999 and has started in the TRIPs Council.

The article allows countries to exclude from patentability plants and animals and essentially biological processes for the production of plants and animals, but makes it compulsory for countries to patent microorganisms and microbiological and nonbiological processes. It also mandates that countries patent plant varieties or set up a sui generis system of protection.

The problems with this article are the following: (i) it does not make scientific sense to distinguish between microorganisms (which must be patentable) and plants and animals (which can be excluded) as all are life forms and should not be allowed to be patented; (ii) it does not make scientific sense to mandate the patenting of microbiological processes, because they are also natural processes; (iii) there is ambiguity about the sui generis system option for plant varieties. The concern of NGOs is that the article will facilitate the patenting of all life forms and the patenting of plant varieties, or the strict protection of plant breeders' rights, at the expense of small farmers.

To correct the serious problems, the review process could lead to amendments of Article 27.3(b), clarifying that (i) no life forms can be patented; (ii) no natural processes for producing plants and animals can be patented; (iii) a sui generis system can include national laws that recognize and protect the traditional knowledge of indigenous and local communities, in line with the Convention on Biological Diversity.

Agriculture and Food Security

In most developing countries, small farmers form a large part of the population. Their livelihoods and products (especially food) are the main basis of Third World economies. These livelihoods could be threatened by agricultural liberalization under the WTO's AOA. Local food production could also be threatened by cheaper imports. Developing countries could then become more dependent on imports for their food supplies, thus eroding national food security.

To deal with these two serious problems, it could be proposed that in developing countries food produced for domestic consumption and the products of small farmers should be exempted from the AOA's disciplines on import liberalization, domestic support, and subsidies.

The TRIMs Agreement

The review of the TRIMs agreement, scheduled to begin in 1999, should highlight the problems of implementation for developing countries. The prohibition of "local content" requirements (i.e., that foreign firms or projects make use of a certain minimum amount of local materials) will seriously hinder the efforts of developing countries to promote local industry, save on foreign exchange, and upgrade local technological capacity. There is also a prohibition on investment measures that limit the import of inputs by firms to a certain percentage of their exports. Such measures had been introduced to protect the countries' balance of payments. The prohibition of these two investment measures will make the attainment of development goals much more difficult.

The TRIMs review should conclude with an amendment to allow developing countries the right to have "local content" policy and to limit the import of inputs to a certain percentage of a firm's exports.

THE PRESSURE FOR NEW ISSUES

A. DANGERS OF THE PROLIFERATION OF "TRADE-RELATED ISSUES"
THE URUGUAY ROUND has already introduced new areas into the trading system, vastly expanding its scope. In recent years, the developed countries have intensified the pressures to incorporate more and more issues that are to their advantage into the WTO. This is being resisted by many developing countries, on the grounds that (i) they are not ready for negotiations on yet more new issues because they are already unable to grapple with the problems generated by the Uruguay Round, (ii) the proposed issues are not in their interests but instead could seriously harm their economies should they become the subject of new WTO

rules; and (iii) the issues are not directly related to trade and do not belong in the WTO.

A long list of "new issues" is being put forward by the northern governments to link trade (and the possible use of trade measures and sanctions as enforcement mechanisms) to several economic and noneconomic areas. Three working groups have been created to examine trade and investment, trade and competition policy, and government procurement. Trade and environment is already being negotiated under the WTO's Committee on Trade and Environment. There have been strong attempts by some northern governments (especially the United States and France) to link trade with labor standards in the WTO. It is possible that efforts will be made to link a wide range of other issues, such as human rights, tax systems, and culture to trade measures in the WTO in the future.

In the Uruguay Round, the issues of investment and IPRs were introduced on the grounds that they were "related to trade." In fact, the real objective was to link the chosen issues to the threat of "trade retaliation and penalties" for noncompliance with disciplines. The device of bringing in new topics by alleging that they are trade-related continues to be used in ongoing WTO negotiations. In fact, the pretense of being directly trade-related is no longer even necessary and may unnecessarily restrict the scope of the issues being introduced. The prefix "trade-related" has now been dropped in proposals for these new issues, which are now sought to be brought into the trade arena through simply using the word "and," as in "trade and environment," "trade and labor standards," "trade and investment," and "trade and competition policy."

The device of linking trade with other issues (when the intention is really to link the dispute settlement system of the WTO to new policy areas) is being increasingly used for the purpose of further opening up Third World economies or to reduce their competitiveness in the scramble for world market shares. The WTO could also be used as an instrument to shift a great portion of the burden of future global economic adjustment (for instance, because of environmental imperatives) to the South, which presently has a very weak bargaining and negotiating position in the WTO forum.

B. THE PROPOSED NEW ISSUES AND DANGERS FOR THE SOUTH

THE EUROPEAN UNION, backed by Japan, Canada, and other developed nations, has announced that it wants to launch a new, post-Seattle round of trade negotiations. They hope that in such a round several issues will be made the subject of negotiations for new multilateral agreements that will be legally binding on WTO members.

Although the United States originally seemed cool to the idea (preferring to push issues it liked on a sector-by-sector basis), it may eventually agree to go along with the proposals for initiating negotiations on at least some of the proposed new issues.

A few developing countries, such as India, Egypt, and Malaysia, spoke up strongly against a new round, with new issues thrown in. Many other developing countries, especially in Africa, have supported this position. They believe that instead of injecting new issues, the WTO should allow developing countries (who, after all, form the majority of the membership of the WTO) the time and space to tackle the problems of implementing the existing agreements. Despite such opposition by these countries, it is unclear whether enough of them will be able to withstand the intense pressures to put the new issues on the agenda.

The main categories of the new issues being proposed are international investment rules, competition policy, and government procurement. These three issues were put on the agenda of the first WTO Ministerial Conference in Singapore in 1996. Most developing countries were against having any negotiations for agreements on these issues, but the pressure from the developed countries was so strong that they compromised and agreed to take part in "working groups" to discuss the issues.

The developing countries made it clear that the working groups had the mandate only to discuss the topics in a sort of academic way, in what was called an "educative process." The working groups had no mandate to start negotiations for agreements.

The three working groups have now gone through almost three years of discussion, during which some of the developed countries made it clear they intend to "upgrade" the talks into negotiations. Their plan now is to use the device of the Millennium Round to make the three issues (investment, competition, and government procurement) the subject of talks for new agreements.

Many countries are also proposing that "industrial tariffs" (the reduction of import duties on manufactured products) be another new issue for negotiations. Although there have, of course, been several previous negotiating rounds on tariff cutting in this sector, the issue is nevertheless considered "new" in that fresh negotiations on the industrial sector are not mandated in the WTO agreements. Thus, a decision to negotiate on this issue would mean a fresh commitment on the part of its members.

Some of the developed countries are also proposing that trade and environment and labor standards be part of the proposed new round. The governments of these countries want to satisfy environmental groups and labor unions that have been protesting the negative effects of free trade. If the environmental and labor standards are also thrown into the pot of the new round, influential civic groups may then be won over, or at least they may not campaign so hard against the proposed round.

The United States, meanwhile, is very keen that the Uruguay Round issues of services, agriculture, and intellectual property rights be revisited and revised so that its corporations will have yet more market openings or advantages. New negotiations on these existing topics, which are already on the WTO agenda in any case, will also certainly be part of a new stage of negotiations, whether or not the new issues are accepted as part of a round.

THE DANGERS OF FOUR NEW ISSUES: INVESTMENT, COMPETITION, GOVERNMENT PROCUREMENT, AND INDUSTRIAL TARIFFS

THE THREE ISSUES that should especially worry developing countries are investment, competition policy, and government procurement. If there is a new round, it could lead to new WTO agreements on these topics. Another round of cuts in industrial tariffs would also pose dangers to developing countries.

The following is a summary of how these issues will affect the developing nations.

A. THE INVESTMENT ISSUE

ON THIS ISSUE, the rich countries are pushing to introduce rules that give new rights to foreign investors, making it easier for them to enter countries and to operate freely. Pressures would be mounted on WTO member states to liberalize investment flows and to grant "national treatment" to foreign investors and firms. Governments would lose a large part of their present rights to regulate the operations of foreign investors. Restrictions on the free flow of capital into and out of the country would be prohibited. Moreover, the "performance requirements" that host governments now place on foreign companies (such as technology transfer, and the use of local professionals) would come under pressure. There is even talk of prohibiting the use of incentives to attract foreign investments.

The recent proposal by the EU to expand investment negotiations in the WTO is a watered-down version of the discredited Multilateral Agreement on Investment (MAI) that the developed countries had negotiated in the OECD. The original OECD-MAI model defined foreign investment to include both short-term flows and foreign direct investment, and gave rights to foreign investors to enter any country (i.e., "pre-establishment rights"), to own 100 percent equity, and to be automatically given "national treatment." Due mainly to public protests, the MAI negotiations collapsed, and the EU has taken a lead in getting negotiations for an investment agreement started at the WTO through the Seattle Ministerial.

Implicitly acknowledging that an MAI replica would be politically unacceptable both to many developing countries and to global civil society, the EU has proposed a diluted version. This would allow countries options on the degree of liberalization and "national treatment" to offer on a sector-by-sector basis, and would be limited to direct foreign investment. It is obvious, however, that this is a tactical move to make their proposal more acceptable. Once such a watered-down version enters the WTO, pressures will then pile on to get the developing countries to liberalize more and more and to offer national treatment.

The entrance in principle of investment policy per se in the WTO would tremendously expand the mandate and powers of the WTO and pose a serious threat to developing countries. Investment liberalization in the South is an objective intensely pursued by the developed countries, just as trade liberalization has been so ruthlessly pursued. Eventually, if the North gets what it wants, developing countries will no longer be able to defend the viability of, or give preferences to, local investors, firms, or farmers, which are all much smaller than the transnational companies, and will thus be unable to withstand the latter's onslaught. They will face the threat of having their local products wiped out by competition from the bigger foreign firms, or of being taken over by them.

B. THE COMPETITION ISSUE

THE EU ARGUES that what it considers to be the core principles of the WTO (national treatment and nondiscrimination) should be applied through a new agreement that would look unfavorably on domestic laws or practices that favor local firms, on the grounds that this is against free competition. For example, policies that give importing or distribution rights (or more favorable rights) to local firms (including government agencies or enterprises) or practices among local firms that give them superior marketing channels are likely to be called into question and disciplines may be imposed on them. The developed countries are arguing that such policies or practices create a barrier to foreign products or firms, which should be allowed to compete on equal terms as locals in the name of free competition.

Developing countries may argue that if these smaller enterprises are treated on a par with the huge foreign conglomerates, most of them would not be able to survive. Perhaps some would remain because over the years (or generations) they have built up distribution systems, based on their intimate knowledge of the local scene, that give them an edge over the more endowed foreign firms. But the operation of such local distribution channels could also come under attack by a competition policy in the WTO, because the developed countries are likely to pressure the local firms to also open their marketing channels to foreign competitors.

At present, many developing countries would argue that giving favorable treatment to locals is procompetitive, in that the smaller local firms are given some advantages to withstand the might of foreign giants, which otherwise would monopolize the local market. Providing the giant international firms equal rights would overwhelm local enterprises, which are small- and medium-sized in global terms.

However, such arguments will not be accepted by the developed countries, which will insist that their giant firms be provided a "level playing field" to compete "equally" with the smaller local firms. They would like their interpretation of "competition" (which, ironically, would likely lead to foreign monopolization of developing country markets) to be enshrined in WTO law through a new round.

In the WTO's Competition Working Group, developing countries have raised issues that are more relevant to them, including the restrictive practices of transnational companies and abuse of antidumping measures by the United States and other developed countries. However, such extremely relevant and legitimate concerns under the topic of "competition" have not been welcomed, especially by the United States. Given the relatively weak negotiating position of the South, the interpretation of developed countries is more likely to prevail, should there be a decision to begin negotiations for a competition agreement in the WTO. This would give another instrument to the developed countries to pry open the markets of the developing countries.

C. THE ISSUE OF GOVERNMENT PROCUREMENT

THE DEVELOPED COUNTRIES want to introduce a process in the WTO whereby their companies would be able to obtain a large share of the lucrative business of providing supplies to and winning contracts for public-sector projects in the developing countries.

At present, such government expenditure is outside the scope of the WTO, unless a member country voluntarily joins the "pluri-lateral" agreement on government procurement. This means that governments are free to set up their own rules on procurement and project awards, and most developing countries give preferences to locals.

The aim of the rich countries is to bring the government spending policies, decisions, and procedures of all member countries under the umbrella of the WTO, where the principle of "national treatment" (foreigners to be treated on a par with or better than locals) will apply. Under this principle, governments in their procurement and contracts for projects (and probably also for privatization deals) would no longer be able to give preferences or advantages to local citizens or firms. The bids for supplies, contracts, and projects would have to be opened up to foreigners, who should be given the same (or better) chances as locals. It is even proposed that foreign firms that are unhappy with the government's decisions be allowed to bring the matter to court in the WTO.

These changes would have a tremendous impact, given that the value of government procurement expenditure in some countries is larger than the value of imports.

As most developing countries would object to having their public-sector spending policies changed so drastically, the developed countries have a two-stage plan for this issue: first, to have an agreement limited to achieving greater "transparency" in government procurement; and second, to have a broader agreement that would cover the aspects of liberalization, market access for foreign firms, and the national treatment principle. Stage one would inject the procurement issue into the WTO multilateral system. Stage two would seek to "fully integrate" government procurement into the WTO system.

At the WTO Seattle Ministerial, the United States will try to wrap up an agreement on "transparency in government procurement." This would allow governments to still favor local firms, but require them to make public (to the WTO members) what they are purchasing and the projects they are opening up for awards, including eligibility criteria for bids and project terms. After such an interim agreement is obtained, the developed countries will then push for an expansion of the agreement, so that it incorporates the market access element, i.e., that foreign firms be given national treatment.

By agreeing now to a negotiation for a transparency agreement, developing countries would also put themselves on the road to a full-scale procurement agreement incorporating liberalization and national treatment. At stake is the right of governments to reserve some of their business for local firms. With the removal of that right, a very important instrument for assisting local firms, for national development, and for socio-economic objectives would be removed.

D. INDUSTRIAL TARIFFS

BESIDES THE THREE ISSUES of investment, competition, and procurement, another economic issue that is being pushed for in the WTO is "industrial tariffs." This would entail another round of negotiations to further reduce duties on manufactured products. Since the tariffs in this sector are generally lower in the developed countries, a new round of tariff cuts would mainly entail new commitments by the developing countries.

Most developing countries have already significantly reduced their tariffs on industrial products in recent years. Many did this under the structural adjustment programs directed by the IMF and the World Bank. An influential study by the UN Economic Commission for Africa on the effects of structural adjustment policies in 1991 warned that: "External trade liberalization for underdeveloped economies can have some serious side effects. For one, it can lead to dumping of cheap products from outside such as clothes, shoes, creams, etc. This undermines the local industries that produce or those that would have started to produce these products as they cannot compete with similar but much cheaper products from abroad. So African infant industries fail to take off under extensive trade liberalization."

In recent years, many African and Latin American countries have suffered from "de-industrialization," a process in which local industries and enterprises have been closed or taken over as they are made noncompetitive by rival imported products.

A further round of cuts in industrial tariffs, as proposed by the developed countries, would render the industrial sector and industrial enterprises of most developing countries even more nonviable. The future of industrialization, especially that based on the survival and development of local enterprises, is at stake in the South.

Therefore, there should not be another formal round of negotiations to further cut developing countries' tariffs. If there is a next stage of negotiations, it should only involve "tariff peaks" (high tariffs) and "tariff escalation" (the practice of imposing no tariffs, or low tariffs, on raw materials but progressively higher tariffs on products that are processed or manufactured from the same raw materials). The developed countries should commit themselves to reducing their tariff peaks and tariff escalation, and not use the promise of this as a carrot to draw in the developing countries to cut the latter's industrial tariffs in a new round.

OTHER ISSUES AT THE DOOR: ENVIRONMENT AND LABOR

A. Social and Environment Issues Seeking an Entrance
ANOTHER SET OF "NEW ISSUES" is knocking on the door to enter the WTO system. Unlike other "new issues" that are pushed by the northern-based corporations, this set of issues is being advocated by social organizations (mainly in the North but also by some in the South) that are seeking ways to protect or promote their interests. The key issues in this category are environment and labor. There may be attempts in the future to

introduce other issues, such as human rights and gender equity. Indeed, if environment and labor were to enter the WTO system as subjects for agreements, it would be conceptually difficult to argue why other social and cultural issues should also not enter.

The objectives of the social organizations in linking their particular causes to trade measures are different from the aims of corporations who seek linkages (in investment and procurement) to gain greater market access and market share, or (in IPRs) to protect their domination and hinder potential new rivals. The social organizations are looking for more effective ways to protect their interests and believe that the instruments of trade measures or trade sanctions can be very effective. They believe that their causes (to defend animal rights, conserve the environment, or protect jobs and promote higher social standards) can most effectively be promoted if governments of countries that have "low environmental and social standards" are faced with the potential threat of trade measures and sanctions on products that are produced using the low standards.

In this, the social organizations concerned are seeking methods similar to those of the corporations, in that they are pressuring their governments and negotiators to make use of a strong enforcement mechanism (unilateral trade measures, or the dispute settlement mechanism of the WTO backed up with the possibility of trade sanctions).

Thus, trade measures have become methods of choice, and the WTO has become a vehicle of choice, for big corporations and some social organizations in promoting their interests.

B. TRADE AND THE ENVIRONMENT

THAT THERE ARE LINKS between trade and the environment cannot and should not be denied. Trade can contribute to environmentally harmful activities. Ecological damage, by making production unsustainable, can also have negative effects on long-term production and trade prospects. In some circumstances, trade (for example, trade in environmentally sound technology products) can assist in improving the environment.

What is of concern or relevance in looking at "linkages" is the advocacy of the use of trade measures and sanctions on environmental grounds. Some environmental and animal rights groups believe that national governments should be given the right to unilaterally impose import bans on products on the grounds that the process of production is destructive and that WTO rules should be amended to enable these unilateral actions.

Some groups, and some developed country members of the WTO, go further and have advocated a set of concepts linking trade measures in the WTO to the environment. These concepts are processes and production methods (PPMs), internalization of environmental costs, and eco-dumping. The three concepts are interrelated. The implication is that if a country has lower environmental standards in an industry or sector, the cost of that country's product is not internalized, making prices artificially low. Thus, when that country exports these products, it is practicing eco-dumping. As a result, an importing country would have the right to impose trade penalties, such as levying countervailing duties, on the goods.

This set of ideas poses complex questions relating to concepts, estimations, and practical application, particularly as they relate to the international setting and to the WTO. Developing countries are likely to find themselves at a great disadvantage within the negotiating context of the WTO, should the subject (which has already been discussed in the Committee on Trade and Environment) come up for negotiations.

One of the main issues is whether all countries should be expected to adhere to the same standard, or whether standards should be allowed to correspond to levels of development. The application of a single standard would be inequitable because poorer countries can ill afford high standards; thus, their products would become noncompetitive. The global burden of adjustment to a more ecological world would be skewed inequitably toward the developing countries.

This is counter to the principle of "common but differentiated responsibility" of the UNCED or Earth Summit, which states that the developed countries, which take the greater share of blame for the ecological crisis and have more means to counter it, should correspondingly bear the greater responsibility for the global costs of adjustment.

Given the unequal bargaining strengths of the North and South in the WTO, the complex issues relating to PPMs, cost internalization, and trade-related environmental measures should not be negotiated within the WTO. If they are discussed at all, the venue should be the United Nations (for example, in the framework of the Commission on Sustainable Development) in which the broader perspective of environment and development and of the UNCED can be brought to bear.

Unilateral trade measures taken by an importing country against a product on the grounds of its production method or process are also fraught with the dangers of protectionism and the penalizing of developing countries. However tempting the route of unilateral import bans may be for the environmental cause, it is an inappropriate route as it will lead to many consequences and could eventually even be counter-productive.

Policies and measures to resolve environmental problems (and there are many such genuine problems that have reached the crisis stage) should be negotiated in international environmental forums and agreements. These measures can include (and have included) trade measures. However, the relationship between the WTO and the multilateral environmental agreements (MEAs) is the subject of much debate. On the one hand, developing countries fear that a system of blanket and automatic approval by the WTO of trade measures adopted by an MEA could lead to abuse and protectionism. A sticking point is what constitutes an MEA, as it may include not only truly international agreements convened by the UN and enjoying near-universal consensus, but also agreements drafted by a few countries that then invite others to join.

On the other hand, environmental groups and also developing country and some developed country governments genuinely fear that negotiations in new MEAs can be (and are being) undermined by the WTO. For example, a few countries argued against an International Biosafety Protocol on the grounds that WTO free-trade principles take precedence over environmental objectives. Such arguments are false, as the WTO already allows for trade measures agreed to in MEAs through the present Article XX. Nevertheless, this tactic was used to reject the proposals by the overwhelming majority of delegations to establish checks on the trade in genetically modified organisms and products. Blatant use of the slogan "free trade" to undermine vital health and environmental concerns contributes to the erosion of public confidence in free trade and the WTO system.

For many NGOs (especially in the South) as well as developing country WTO members, an important "trade and environment" issue is the effect of the TRIPs agreement in hindering access to environmentally sound technologies and products. There can be "synergy" between liberalization, environment, and development objectives if TRIPs is amended to enable exemptions for environmentally sound technology. Also, Article 27.3(b) of TRIPs opens the road to the patenting of life forms, a development with numerous potential adverse effects:

- facilitation of the appropriation of traditional knowledge on the use of biological resources by corporations that claim to meet the patent test
- promotion of environmentally harmful technologies and

◆ promotion of technologies that are against the interests of small farmers (such as the "terminator seeds" engineered not to reproduce themselves, so that farmers are prevented from saving seeds).

These are examples of some issues that can and should be taken up in trade and environmental reviews of various agreements.

In short, discussions within the WTO entailing the environmental effects of WTO rules can be beneficial, provided that the environment is viewed within the context of sustainable development, with the critical component of development being given adequate weight. But there should not be any move to initiate an "environmental agreement" in the WTO that involves concepts such as PPMs and eco-dumping.

C. TRADE AND LABOR STANDARDS

The push for incorporating labor standards with trade measures in the WTO has come from labor unions in the North and international trade unions that also have affiliations in developing countries. However, some trade unions in some developing countries are opposed to including labor standards in the WTO. Proponents have linked the issue of labor standards to the broader concept of a "social clause," which could include the rights of various groups in society. Some political parties in developed countries also support this concept.

Advocates of a social clause may be motivated by various objectives. Many trade unions believe that transnational corporations are relocating from countries with higher labor standards to those with lower standards, and that this trend acts to depress labor standards by reducing the bargaining power of workers. They also believe that by linking the threat of trade sanctions to labor standards, there will be pressure to upgrade the level of standards in developing countries. They are careful to include only internationally recognized core labor standards and to exclude the issue of wage levels in the demands for linkage to trade and the WTO.

Other advocates believe that the linking of social issues (including, but not exclusively, labor standards) to the WTO and its sanctions system of enforcement is an effective way of countering the adverse social effects of trade and investment liberalization, by forcing corporations and governments to observe socially responsible policies.

Developing countries fear that the objectives of the northern and international trade unions, and of developed country governments that back the social clause demand, are mainly protectionist in nature, that they want to protect jobs in the North by reducing the low-cost incentive that attracts global corporations to developing countries. They argue that low labor costs in their countries are a function not of deliberate exploitation of workers but of the general low standard of living and the lower level of development, and that the low cost is a legitimate comparative advantage. They therefore have opposed the inclusion of labor standards in the WTO and argued successfully (as in the Singapore Ministerial Declaration) that the issue belongs in the ILO.

There is, of course, justification for public interest groups to be concerned about the social consequences of globalization and liberalization and to campaign to change the nature and effects of the present globalization trends. However, the issue is whether labor standards and social clauses in trade agreements are an appropriate route. Arguments to the contrary have merit for the following reasons:

i.   Such an issue, when placed in the WTO context, would be linked to the dispute settlement system and the remedy of trade penalties and sanctions. In other venues, there is the option (which many would argue is more appropriate) of linking the improving of labor standards to positive incentives, rather than seeking punitive measures.

ii. Even though most advocates only demand minimum labor standards such as the right of association for workers, there is no certainty that the issue will be so confined in the future. Once the concept of social issues and rights enters the WTO system, it can be expanded within the particular issue (e.g., an extension to social security and wage levels within the issue of labor standards) and extended to other issues (such as the rights of children, women, and the disabled; human rights in general; the right to education, health, nutrition, etc).

iii. It is possible or even likely that once rights and social issues enter the WTO, countries with low social standards would be deemed to be practicing "social dumping" (or unfairly subsidizing its products by avoiding social costs) and importing countries could be enabled to impose countervailing duties.

iv. Developing countries are likely to bear the costs of a loss of competitiveness. The poor social conditions in the poorer countries are largely related to the low level of development and the lack of resources (although the waste and mismanagement of resources also do contribute significantly). Lower social standards are thus linked to (though not entirely caused by) lower levels of development. It is very possible that the linkage between social standards and trade measures in the WTO system would lead to placing additional pressures on developing countries and that many of their products would cost more and become noncompetitive, or face trade penalties, or both.

v. It is possible that the firms and products eventually affected will not be confined to those involving trade and exports but would include the firms (most of them small and locally owned) that cater to the local market. By not being able to remain competitive, some might close.

vi. It is also possible that the erosion of competitiveness and the higher costs (perhaps beyond what would normally prevail in countries at the existing stage of development) would cause loss of jobs, closure of firms and farms, and reduced investment; or the movement of some workers to more poorly paid jobs.

vii. The inclusion of labor standards would open the door to a much wider range of issues relating to social standards, social rights, and human rights. Many new "conditionalities" would be introduced, not only on trade at the border but also on domestic production and investment. The issues will be so complex and complicated that they will tie the WTO system in knots, and occupy the time and energy of diplomats and policy makers, not to mention the NGOs and social organizations, in an enterprise that is fraught with controversies and dangers, and with no clear guaranteed benefits.

viii. Finally, the efforts of NGOs and social organizations could be directed instead toward the sources of the social problems within and outside the WTO. For example, to offset problems caused by the WTO, those concerned about human rights and the livelihood rights of ordinary people could examine and campaign for changes to the existing agreements (such as TRIPs and TRIMs and those on agriculture and services). They could also try to prevent new agreements (such as those on investment, procurement, and industrial tariffs) that would affect the viability of local firms, the livelihoods of workers, and the people's right to development.

And to counter problems whose sources are beyond the WTO, there can be intensified campaigns for debt relief and reforms to the IMF and structural adjustment programs, a proemployment macroeconomic policy (rather than priority to restrictive monetary policy), as well as campaigns for improved human rights and against exploitative child labor and poor working conditions, etc. But the notion that linking social rights to a trade sanctions regime, though tempting at first, is likely to be counterproductive in results.

CONCLUSION

THIS SURVEY OF THE WTO from a southern perspective shows how the developing and the poor countries are continuously being disadvantaged by the WTO, its rules, and its system. The system itself upholds the weak bargaining position of the South and the grave inequities in negotiating capacities.

In the recent past, this has already led to many agreements in the WTO that reflect the inequities on the negotiating table. The WTO agreements and rules themselves are inequitable and unbalanced, and in many respects place developing countries not only at a disadvantage or in a marginalized position, but also place them in danger of losing their economic sovereignty, their development prospects, and their food security.

Yet, if anything, the WTO is not a static organization. Among its main functions is further and continuous negotiations, with the intention to make more rules, and to monitor (and if necessary, to ensure the enforcement of) the implementation of existing agreements. The WTO can also review existing rules and amend them to offset their deficiencies and weaknesses.

It is thus possible for the WTO to focus its energies on correcting the present inequities and imbalances both in its rules and its process. Indeed, this is already on the agenda of the WTO since the problems of implementation and a review of many of the agreements are mandated for discussion as part of the WTO's work in the next few years.

The past many years have seen a program of very intense negotiations that have expanded the GATT system's scope of issues and propelled the WTO into the forefront of international organizations. WTO developments have been at such an accelerated pace that policy makers, diplomats, parliamentarians, NGOs, civil society, and scholars have all failed to keep abreast of them, analyze them, and implement national policies and laws to conform to the them, as well as assess the serious implications of this compliance.

The WTO has, in a very few years, stamped a new paradigm for national economic and social policies worldwide, and a new framework of international economic relations. The more that one understands the paradigm, the more serious are the questions raised on where the WTO is leading our societies.

From the viewpoint of civil society worldwide, and especially from the South, the next few years must see the WTO engaged in a serious review and repair of its rules, process, and system. However, the commerce departments and trade ministries of the rich countries do not seem to share this priority. They represent the short-term views and interests of their large corporations, which are obsessed with obtaining more rights for themselves, getting governments to remove whatever little restrictions are left on their behavior, and gaining more trade and investment access to the markets, natural resources, and territories of the developing world.

Thus, the biggest pressures are for more "new issues" to be added to the WTO. If these new issues enter, the multilateral trading system will balloon even further, taking on a load that may cause it to sink. But before that happens, many countries and many people will be subjected to even greater pressures, which can be expected to lead to economic and social disintegration and political chaos.

The people of developing countries will be the main victims of a further distortion of world trade. But people everywhere will suffer as this trend further widens the gap between rich and poor and between weak and powerful; undermines environmental protection; channels control over biodiversity, food, and natural resources to a few transnational corporations; and erodes economic and social sovereignty.

The operational principles of the WTO urgently need an

overhaul. Its present assumption is that whatever hinders total trade and investment liberalization is "distortive" and should be removed, and that the WTO's mission is to lead this process of removal. This concept itself is a distortion of reality. For developing countries, weak enterprises, and small farms, such liberalization has already caused closure and dislocation. The development process requires that a liberalization policy can only be pursued on a selective basis, at a pace that corresponds with the strengthening of the capacity of such enterprises and farms and of the developing countries themselves.

Pressuring and forcing countries to liberalize trade and investment before they can sensibly or practically do it is the real distortion of the multilateral trading system. The sooner the political leaders and trade representatives of developed countries realize this, the better. Otherwise, with their control of the system, they will continue to lead the WTO in the wrong direction and on a road with a bleak future strewn with countries, communities, and people victimized by economic and social disintegration and environmental destruction.

Note: This paper draws on some previous articles by the author, some of which are listed in the references.

REFERENCES

Das, Bhagirath Das (1998), *The WTO Agreements: Deficiencies, Imbalances and Required Changes*. Third World Network, Penang.

Das, Bhagirath Das (1999), *Some Suggestions for Improvements in the WTO Agreements*. Third World Network, Penang.

Khor, Martin (1997). The WTO and the South. Third World Network briefing paper.

Khor, Martin (1999). *A Comment on Attempted Linkages between Trade and Non-Trade Issues in the WTO*. Paper.

Khor, Martin (1999). *Civil society's interaction with the WTO*. Paper.

Khor, Martin (1999). *Dangers in a Proposed New Round of the World Trade Organization*. Paper.

Raghavan, Chakravarthi (1990). *Recolonisation*. Third World Network, Penang.

BUILDING AN IRON CAGE: THE BRETTON WOODS INSTITUTIONS, THE WTO, AND THE SOUTH

Walden Bello

Walden Bello is co-director of Focus on the Global South, a Bangkok-based research, analysis, and advocacy program on North-South issues connected with the Chulalongkorn University Social Research Institute. A professor of sociology and public administration at the University of the Philippines, he is author or co-author of ten books, including Siamese Tragedy: Development and Disintegration in Modern Thailand *(London: Zed Press, 1998);* Dark Victory: The United States, Structural Adjustment, and Global Poverty *(London: Pluto Press, 1994); and* Dragons in Distress: Asia's Miracle Economies in Crisis *(London: Penguin Books, 1991).*

In this paper, Walden Bello places the WTO in a historical context saying that this institution represents the culmination of a long campaign by northern countries to contain the development aspirations of the South. He describes the North's tactics over the past five decades to obstruct the efforts of developing nations to pursue their interests through the United Nations system or by other means. Bello also dissects current WTO agreements that are likely to have a devastating impact on the Third World, such as those on intellectual property and agriculture, and he concludes with a strategy for change. This involves preserving the legitimacy of the UN system, while demanding profound alternatives in the policies and processes of the WTO and the International Monetary Fund, if they are to be preserved at all.

S UPPORTERS OF THE World Trade Organization (WTO) often claim that this multilateral institution protects weaker and poorer countries from unilateral actions by the stronger ones by providing a set of uniform rules and dispute settlement mechanisms for global trade. Nevertheless, the WTO elicits fear, anger, and exasperation throughout the global South, where it is widely believed that this institution, rather than helping to level the playing field, is deeply biased against the development of the South. This bias was recently epitomized for many by the resistance of key northern countries, led by the United States, to the appointment of Thai Deputy Prime Minister Supachai Panitchpakdi as WTO director general.

This southern attitude toward the WTO can best be appreciated if the emergence of the institution is placed in the context of the South's struggle for development over the last 50 years. Situated in this broad historical canvas, the Uruguay Round Agreement of 1994 emerges not so much as the triumph of enlightened free trade over benighted protectionism but, more importantly, as the culminating point of a campaign of global economic containment of the legitimate aspirations to development on the part of Third World countries.

Earlier milestones in this process were:

◆ the reorientation of the World Bank toward managing development in the South in the late 1950s

◆ the IMF's new role as the watchdog of the Third World countries' external economic relations in the 1970s

◆ the universalization of structural adjustment in the 1980s

◆ and the unilateralist trade campaign waged against the Asian "tiger economies" by Washington beginning in the early 1980s.

This is not to say that the struggle between advanced industrial countries around the issue of free trade or protection was not a central driving force for the establishment of the WTO. It definitely was. It is to assert, however, that containing the South was an equally key dynamic that intersected crucially with the fight for markets among the developed countries.

THE 1950S THROUGH THE 1970S: EMERGENCE OF THE SOUTHERN AGENDA

THE PLACE TO BEGIN this analysis is the period of decolonization in the 1950s and 1960s. The emergence of scores of newly independent states took place in the politically charged atmosphere of the Cold War, but although they were often split between East and West in their political alliances, Third World countries gravitated toward an economic agenda that had two underlying thrusts: rapid development and a global redistribution of wealth.

While the more radical expression of this agenda in the form of the Leninist theory of imperialism drew much attention and, needless to say, condemnation in some quarters, it was the more moderate version that was most influential in drawing otherwise politically diverse Third World governments into a common front. This was the vision, analysis, and program of action forged by Raul Prebisch, an Argentine economist who, from his base at the United Economic Commission for Latin America (CEPAL), won a global following with his numerous writings. Developed in the late 1950s and early 1960s, Prebisch's theory centered on the worsening terms of trade between industrialized and non-industrialized countries, which resulted in the South needing to use more and more of its raw materials and agricultural products to purchase fewer and fewer of the North's manufactured products. Moreover, the trading relationship was likely to get worse because northern producers were developing substitutes for raw materials from the South, and northern consumers, according to Engels' Law, would spend a decreasing proportion of their income on agricultural products from the South.

Known in development circles as "structuralism," Prebisch's theory of what one writer described as "bloodless but inexorable exploitation" served as the inspiration for Third World organizations, formations, and programs that sprang up in the 1960s and 1970s. These included the Non-Aligned Movement, the Group of 77, Organization of Petroleum Exporting Countries (OPEC), and the New International Economic Order (NIEO). The structuralist critique was also central to the establishment of the UN Conference on Trade and Development (UNCTAD) in 1964, which became over the next decade the principal vehicle used by the Third World countries in their effort to restructure the world economy.

With Prebisch as its first secretary general, UNCTAD advanced a global reform strategy with three main prongs. The first was commodity price stabilization, through the negotiation of floors below which commodity prices would not be allowed to fall. The second was a scheme of preferential tariffs allowing Third World exports of manufactures, in the name of development, to enter First World markets at lower tariff rates than those applied to exports from other industrialized countries. The third was an expansion and acceleration of foreign assistance, which, in UNCTAD's view, was not charity but "compensation, a rebate to the Third World for the years of declining commodity purchasing power." UNCTAD also sought to gain legitimacy for the southern countries' use of protectionist trade policy as a mechanism for industrialization and demanded accelerated transfer of technology to the South.

To varying degrees, the structuralist critique came to be

reflected in the approaches of other key economic agencies of the United Nations secretariat, such as the Economic and Social Council (ECOSOC) and the United Nations Development Program (UNDP), and it became the dominant viewpoint among the majority at the General Assembly.

A. THE BRETTON WOODS INSTITUTIONS FOCUS ON THE SOUTH

THE RESPONSE OF THE LEADING countries of the North to the emerging countries' challenge of economic decolonization was conditioned by several developments. Most important of these was the Cold War. The priority of the political enterprise of containing the Soviet Union and Communism pushed the North, particularly the U.S. government, to a less hardline stance when it came to the question of whether the economic structures of its client countries conformed to free-market principles. While the United States upheld private enterprise and demanded access for its corporations, it was more tolerant when it came to protectionism, investment controls, and a strong role for government in managing the economy. It also veered away from a classic exploitative stance to promote at least the image of supporting limited global redistribution of wealth, mainly through foreign aid.

As the emerging countries gravitated toward the UN system, the leading governments increasingly relied on the International Monetary Fund (IMF) and the International Bank for Reconstruction and Development (IBRD) to push their agenda. These Bretton Woods institutions, founded in 1944, began with missions quite distinct from those that let to their latter-day involvement with North-South relations. The IMF was conceived by John Maynard Keynes and Harry Dexter White, the two pillars of the Bretton Woods meeting, as the guardian of global liquidity. It was to fulfill this function by monitoring member countries' maintenance of stable exchange rates and providing facilities on which they could periodically draw to overcome cyclical balance of payments difficulties. The IBRD, on the other hand, was, as its name implied, set up to assist in the reconstruction of war-torn economies, particularly those of Western Europe, by lending to them at manageable rates of interest.

By the early 1970s, however, President Nixon's decision to take the dollar off the gold standard had inaugurated a new era of floating exchange rates that made the IMF's original mission superfluous. Instead, the Fund became deeply involved in stabilizing Third World economies with balance of payments difficulties. As for the IBRD (now one component of the World Bank Group), it had evolved into the prime multilateral development agency for aid and development. For this agency, a turning point of sorts was the debate triggered by the 1951 report of a group of experts entitled "Measures for the Economic Development of Under-Developed Countries," which proposed making grant aid available to Third World countries. Using this as a springboard, Third World countries at the General Assembly tried to push for the establishment of a Special UN Fund for Economic Development (Sunfed), which would have been controlled not by the North but by the UN and whose criterion for providing loans would not be narrow banking rules but development need.

The North, led by the United States, strenuously resisted these efforts, resorting at first to delay and diversion, such as proposing the creation of a $100 million fund to be used to finance an investment survey that the IBRD or some other Western agency would undertake. But when these tactics failed to derail the South's drive to set up Sunfed, the North came out with an alternative: an institution for making soft loans for development from capital subscribed by the North but one controlled by the North rather than the Third World majority at the United Nations. Thus came into being the International Development

Association (IDA), which was attached to the World Bank as the latter's soft-loan window. As one analyst of this period has pointed out, much of the impetus for the IDA came from the Bank itself, increasingly worried over southern demands for a competing UN fund. Eugene R. Black, the bank's shrewd president, said bluntly that "the International Development Association was really an idea to offset the urge for Sunfed." Black, like any other banker, had little use for soft loans. But if anybody was going to be making them, he reasoned, it had better be the Bank.

The IDA was part of a compromise package that also included the establishment of the UN Special Fund, later renamed the UN Development Program (UNDP), which served as the channel of much smaller quantities of mainly technical aid to Third World countries.

The IDA-UNDP compromise derailed the demand for a UN-controlled funding agency, but it did not stop the escalation of Third World demands for a redistribution of global economic power. These demands resulted in the establishment of UNC-TAD in 1964, the OPEC countries seizing control of the pricing of oil in the early- and mid-1970s, and the adoption by the UN General Assembly Special Session of 1974 of the program of the "New International Economic Order."

The thrust of these moves was clearly reformist rather than revolutionary, expressing the demands of Third World elites rather than Third World masses. Nevertheless, their prominence in the context of successful struggles waged by revolutionary movements in Vietnam and other Third World countries lent a note of urgency to Washington's search for an effective counter-strategy of managed reform.

B. THE SOUTHERN CHALLENGE IN THE 1970S

IN THE 1970S, the World Bank was to be the centerpiece of liberal Washington's policy toward the global South. Robert

McNamara, appointed World Bank President in 1968 (after a troubled stint at the U.S. Defense Department), developed a three-pronged approach. First was a massive escalation in the World Bank's resources, with McNamara raising World Bank lending from an average of $2.7 billion a year when he took office in 1968, to $8.7 billion in 1978, to $12 billion by the time he left office in 1981. Second was a global program aimed at ending poverty, not by tackling the difficult problems associated with social reform, but by focusing aid on improving the "productivity of the poor." Third was an effort to split the South by picking a few countries as "countries of concentration," to which the flow of bank assistance would be higher than average for countries of similar size and income.

The rise of OPEC, however, made World Bank aid and foreign aid in general less critical to many of the leading countries in UNCTAD and the Group of 77 in the mid-1970s. Suddenly, they had access to massive quantities of loans that the commercial banks were only too happy to make available in their effort to turn a profit on the billions of dollars of deposits made to them by the OPEC countries.

Instead of aid, UNCTAD focused on changing the rules of international trade, and in this enterprise it registered some successes. During the fourth conference of UNCTAD in Nairobi in 1976, agreement was reached, without dissent from the developed countries, on the Integrated Program for Commodities (IPC). The IPC stipulated that agreements for 18 specified commodities would be negotiated or renegotiated with the principal aim of avoiding excessive price fluctuations and keeping prices at levels that would be fair to both producers and consumers. It was also agreed that a Common Fund would be set up that would regulate prices when they either fell below or climbed too far above the negotiated price targets. UNCTAD and Group of 77 pressure was also central to the IMF's establishing a new window, the

Compensatory Financing Facility (CFF), which was meant to assist Third World countries in managing foreign exchange crises created by sharp falls in the prices of the primary commodities they exported. Another UNCTAD achievement was getting the industrialized countries to accept the principle of preferential tariffs for developing countries. Some 26 developed countries were involved in sixteen separate "General System of Preferences" schemes by the early 1980s.

These concessions were, of course, limited. In the case of commodity price stabilization, it soon became apparent that the rich countries had replaced a strategy of confrontation with a Fabian, or evasive, strategy of frustrating concrete agreements. A decade after UNCTAD IV, only one new commodity stabilization agreement, for natural rubber, had been negotiated; an existing agreement on cocoa was not operative; and agreements on tin and sugar had collapsed.

C. RIGHT-WING REACTION AND THE DEMONIZATION OF THE SOUTH

BY THE LATE 1970S, even such small concessions were viewed with alarm by increasingly influential sectors of the U.S. establishment. Such concessions within the UN system were seen in the context of other developments in North-South relations, which appeared to show that the strategy of liberal containment spearheaded by the Bank in the area of economic relations had not produced what it had promised to deliver: security for Western interests in the South through the co-optation of Third World elites.

While professing anticommunism, governing elites throughout the Third World nevertheless angered U.S. business interests by giving in to popular pressure, abetted by local industrial interests, to tighten up on foreign investment. Nowhere did this trend spark more apprehension among American business than in two countries that were considered enormously strategic by U.S. multinational firms—Brazil and Mexico. In Brazil, where foreign-owned firms accounted for half of the total manufacturing sales, the military-technocrat regime, invoking national security considerations, moved in the late 1970s to reserve the strategic information sector to local industries, provoking bitter denunciation from IBM and other U.S. computer firms. In Mexico, where foreign firms accounted for nearly 30 percent of the manufacturing output, U.S. pharmaceutical firms threatened legal actions and divestment when the Mexican government announced proposals for no-patent policies, promotion of generic medicines, local development of raw materials, price controls, discriminatory incentives for local firms, and controls on foreign investment.

Even more disturbing to the United States was OPEC's second "oil shock" in 1979. To many Americans, OPEC became the symbol of the South: an irresponsible gang that was bent on using its near monopoly over a key resource to bring the West to its knees. The "oil weapon" evoked more apprehension than the nuclear arms of the Soviet Union, even though OPEC was dominated by U.S. allies such as Saudi Arabia, Kuwait, and Venezuela. Moreover, American hostility remained focused on the OPEC nations, even though they had as much reason to blame the international oil companies, which maintained high profits throughout the oil shock by passing on the price increase to consumers.

Indeed, the oil cartel was feared as the precursor of a unified southern bloc controlling most strategic commodities. Right-wing propagandists pointed to the Algiers Declaration of the Non-Aligned Movement in 1973 in their efforts to fan fear and loathing in the North. This declaration recommended "the establishment of effective solidarity organizations for the defense of the raw materials producing countries such as the

Organization of Petroleum Export Countries...to recover natural resources and ensure increasingly substantial export earnings."

D. TARGETING THE UN SYSTEM

THE UN SYSTEM was a central feature of the demonology of the South that right-wing circles articulated in the late 1970s and early 1980s. In their view, the UN had become the main vehicle for the South's strategy to bring about the New International Economic Order. As the right-wing think tank Heritage Foundation saw it, the governments of the South devoted "enormous time and resources to spreading the NIEO ideology throughout the UN system and beyond. Virtually no UN agencies and bureaus have been spared." Heritage described what it saw as a concerted effort to redistribute global economic power via UN mechanisms: "Private business data flows are under attack internationally and by individual Third World countries; proposals for strict controls of the international pharmaceutical trade are pending before more than one UN body; other international agencies are drafting restrictive codes of conduct for multinational corporations; and UNESCO has proposed international restraints on the press."

Especially threatening to the Foundation was the effort by the Third World to "redistribute natural resources" by bringing the seabed, space, and Antarctica under their control through the Law of the Sea Treaty, the Agreement Governing Activities of States on the Moon and Other Celestial Bodies (called the "Moon Treaty"), and an ongoing UN study and debate over Antarctica. Malaysian Prime Minister Mahathir Bin Mohamad, the principal architect of the effort to get the UN to claim Antarctica, told the General Assembly "all the unclaimed wealth of this earth" is the "common heritage of mankind" and therefore subject to the political control of the Third World.

THE 1980S AND EARLY 1990S: RESUBORDINATION OF THE SOUTH

A. STRUCTURAL ADJUSTMENT

WHEN THE REAGAN ADMINISTRATION came to power in 1981, it was riding on what it considered a mandate not only to roll back communism but also to discipline the Third World. What unfolded over the next four years was a two-pronged strategy aimed, on the one hand, at dismantling the system of "state-assisted capitalism" that was seen as the domestic base for southern national capitalist elites and, on the other, at drastically weakening the UN system as a forum and instrument for the South's economic agenda. The opportunity came none too soon in the form of the global debt crisis that erupted in the summer of 1982, which drastically weakened the capabilities of Southern governments in dealing with northern states and corporations and northern-dominated multilateral agencies.

The instruments chosen for rolling back the South were the World Bank and the IMF. This was an interesting transformation for the World Bank, which had previously been vilified by the *Wall Street Journal* and the right wing as one of the villains behind the weakening of the North's global position by "promoting socialism" in the Third World via its loans to southern governments. But the liberal McNamara, by that time faulted by the right for losing Vietnam and failing to contain the southern challenge, was replaced by a more pliable successor, and ideological right-wingers seeking the closure of the Bank were restrained by pragmatic conservatives who wished to use the Bank instead as a disciplinary mechanism.

"Structural adjustment" referred to a new lending approach that had been formulated during McNamara's last years at the Bank. Unlike the traditional World Bank project loan, a structural adjustment loan was intended to push a program of "reform" that would cut across the whole economy or a whole sector of the economy. In the mid-1980s, IMF– and World Bank–imposed structural adjustment became the vehicle for a program of free-market liberalization that was applied across the board to Third World economies suffering major debt problems. Almost invariably, structural adjustment programs (SAPs) had the following elements:

♦ radically reducing government spending, ostensibly to control inflation and reduce the demand for capital inflows from abroad, a measure that in practice translated into cutting spending on health, education, and welfare

♦ liberalizing imports and removing restrictions on foreign investment, ostensibly to make local industry more efficient by exposing them to foreign competition

♦ privatizing state enterprises and embarking on radical deregulation in order to promote more efficient allocation and use of productive resources by relying on market mechanisms instead of government decree

♦ devaluing the currency in order to make exports more competitive, thus resulting in more dollars to service the foreign debt and

♦ cutting or constraining wages and eliminating or weakening mechanisms like the minimum wage that protected labor, to remove what were seen as artificial barriers to the mobility of local and foreign capital.

By the late 1980s, more than seventy Third World countries had submitted to IMF and World Bank programs, making stabilization, structural adjustment, and shock therapy from distant Washington the common conditions of the South. The main justification for structural adjustment was to enable Third World countries to repay their debts to northern banks. There was also a more strategic objective, and that was to dismantle the system of state-assisted capitalism that served as the domestic base for the national capitalist elites. In 1988, a survey of SAPs carried out by the UN Commission for Africa concluded that the essence of SAPs was the "reduction/removal of direct state intervention in the productive and redistributive sectors of the economy." As for Latin America, one analyst noted that the United States took advantage of "this period of financial strain to insist that debtor countries remove the government from the economy as the price of getting credit." Similarly, a retrospective of the decade of adjustment published by the Inter-American Development Bank in 1992 identified the removal of the state from economic activity as the centerpiece of the ideological perspective that guided the structural reforms of the 1980s. The book describes the post-war period in Latin America as "the history of a collective error in terms of the economic course chosen, and of the design of the accompanying institutions" and proposed the following remedy: "the withdrawal of the producer state and state-assisted capitalism, the limiting of the state's responsibilities to its constitutional commitments, a return to the market for the supply of goods and services, and the removal of the obstacles to the emergence of an independent entrepreneurial class."

By the end of the twelve-year-long Reagan-Bush era in 1992, the South had been transformed. From Argentina to Ghana, state participation in the economy had been drastically curtailed; government enterprises were passing into private hands in the name of efficiency; protectionist barriers to northern imports were being radically reduced; and, through export-first policies, the internal economy was more tightly integrated into the North-dominated capitalist world markets.

B. BRINGING THE NICs TO HEEL
THERE WAS ONE AREA of the South that was relatively untouched by the first phase of the northern economic counterrevolution.

That was East and Southeast Asia. Here, practically all the economic systems displayed the same features of state-assisted capitalism found elsewhere in the South: an activist government intervening in key areas of the economy, a focus on industrialization in order to escape the fate of being simply agricultural or raw material producers, protection of the domestic market from foreign competition, and tight controls on foreign investment. Where the key East and Southeast Asian economies appeared to differ from other economies in the South was mainly in the presence of a fairly strong state that was able to discipline local elites, the greater internalization of a developmentalist direction by the state elite, and the pursuit of aggressive mercantilist policies aimed at gaining markets in First World countries, particularly the United States.

The frontline status in Asia of many of these so-called "Newly Industrializing Countries" (NICs) during the Cold War ensured that Washington would turn a blind eye to many of their deviations from the free-market ideal. But as the Cold War wound down, the United States began to redefine its economic policy toward East Asia as the creation of a "level playing field" for its corporations via liberalization, deregulation, and more extensive privatization of Asian economies.

It was a goal that Washington pursued by various means in the late 1980s and early 1990s. However, countries like South Korea, Thailand, and Indonesia were able to avoid accepting formal SAPs during the debt crisis because of increased access to Japanese capital. At that time, Japan was relocating many of its industrial operations to East and Southeast Asia to offset the loss of competitiveness in Japan after the 1985 Plaza Accord triggered a rapid appreciation of the yen. This left unilateralism in trade and financial diplomacy as the principal U.S. mechanisms for dealing with the increasingly successful Asian "tigers." Washington's aggressive mood was aptly captured by a senior

U.S. official who told a capital markets conference in San Francisco, "Although the NICs may be regarded as tigers because they are strong, ferocious traders, the analogy has a darker side. Tigers live in the jungle, and by the law of the jungle. They are a shrinking population."

Indeed, unilateral pressure, with some assistance from the IMF and the World Bank, succeeded in getting key Asian countries to liberalize their capital accounts and to move to greater liberalization of their financial sectors. But when it came to trade liberalization, the results were meager, except perhaps in the case of Korea, whose trade surplus with the United States had been turned into a trade deficit by the early 1980s. But even this development did not change the assessment of Korea by the U.S. Trade Representative (USTR) as "one of the toughest places in the world to do business." As for the Southeast Asian countries, Washington's assessment was that while they might have liberalized their capital accounts and financial sectors, they remained highly protected when it came to trade. Some were dangerously flirting with "trade-distorting" exercises in industrial policy, among which were Malaysia's national car project, the Proton Saga, and Indonesia's drive to set up a passenger aircraft industry.

The indiscriminate financial liberalization demanded by Washington and the Bretton Woods institutions, coupled with the high interest rate and fixed currency regime favored by local financial authorities, brought massive amounts of foreign capital into the region. But it also served as the wide highway through which $100 billion exited in 1997 in a massive stampede in response to dislocations caused by overinvestment and unrestricted capital inflows like the collapse of the real estate market and widening current account deficits. A golden opportunity to push the U.S. agenda opened up with the financial crisis, and Washington did not hesitate to exploit it to the hilt, advancing its interests behind the banner of free-market reform. The rollback of protectionism and activist state intervention was incorporated into stabilization programs imposed by the IMF on the key crisis countries of Indonesia, Thailand, and South Korea.

In Thailand, local authorities agreed to remove all limitations on foreign ownership of Thai financial firms, accelerate the privatization of state enterprises, and revise bankruptcy laws along lines demanded by the country's foreign creditors. As the USTR proudly told Congress, the Thai government's "commitments to restructure public enterprises and accelerate privatization of certain key sectors, including energy, transportation, utilities, and communications—which will enhance market-driven competition and deregulation—[are expected] to create new business opportunities for U.S. firms."

In Indonesia, the USTR emphasized that the IMF's conditions for granting a massive stabilization package addressed "practices that have long been the subject of this [Clinton] Administration's bilateral trade policy...Most notable in this respect is the commitment by Indonesia to eliminate the tax, tariff, and credit privileges provided to the national car project. Additionally, the IMF program seeks broad reform of Indonesian trade and investment policy, like the aircraft project, monopolies and domestic trade restrictive practices that stifle competition by limiting access for foreign goods and services."

The national car project and the plan to set up a passenger jet aircraft industry were efforts at industrial policy that had elicited the strong disapproval of Detroit and Boeing, respectively.

In the case of Korea, the U.S. Treasury and the IMF did not conceal their close working relationship, with the Fund clearly in a subordinate position. Not surprisingly, the concessions made by the Koreans were identical to the goals of U.S. bilateral policy toward the country before the crisis. These included raising the limit on foreign ownership of corporate stocks to 55 percent, permitting the establishment of foreign financial institutions, full liberalization of the financial and capital market, abolition of the car classification system, and an end to government-directed lending for industrial policy goals.

As the USTR candidly told members of the U.S. Congress: "Policy-driven rather than market-driven economic activity meant that U.S. industry encountered many specific structural barriers to trade, investment, and competition in Korea. For example, Korea maintained restrictions on foreign ownership and operations, and had a list of market access impediments…The Korea stabilization package, negotiated with the IMF in December 1997, should help open and expand competition in Korea by creating a more market-driven economy…[I]f it continues on the path to reform there will be important benefits not only for Korea but also the United States."

Summing up Washington's strategic goal, Jeff Garten, undersecretary of Commerce during President Clinton's first term, said, "Most of these countries are going through a dark and deep tunnel…But on the other end there is going to be a significantly different Asia in which American firms have achieved a much deeper market penetration, much greater access." By 1998, U.S. financial firms and corporations were buying up Asian assets from Seoul to Bangkok at fire-sale prices.

C. Dismantling the UN Development System

THE ASSAULT ON THE NICs via the IMF stabilization programs and on the broader South via Bretton Woods–imposed structural adjustment was accompanied by a major effort to emasculate the UN as a vehicle for the southern agenda. Wielding the power of the purse, the United States, which funds some 20 to 25 percent of the UN budget, moved to silence NIEO rhetoric in all the key UN institutions dealing with the North-South divide: the Economic and Social Council (ECOSOC), the UNDP, and the General Assembly. U.S. pressure resulted as well in the effective dismantling of the UN Center on Transnational Corporations, whose high-quality work in tracking the activities of global firms in the South had earned the ire of the corporate community. Also abolished was the post of director general for International Economic Cooperation and Development, which had been among the few concrete outcomes, and certainly the most note-worthy, of the efforts of the developing countries to secure a stronger UN presence in support of international economic cooperation and development.

But the focus of the northern counteroffensive was the defang-ing, if not dismantling, of UNCTAD. After giving in to the South during the UNCTAD IV negotiations in Nairobi in 1976 by agreeing to the creation of the commodity stabilization scheme known as the Integrated Program for Commodities, the North, during UNCTAD V in Belgrade, refused the South's program of debt forgiveness and other measures intended to revive Third World economies and thus contribute to global recovery at a time of worldwide recession. The northern offensive escalated during UNCTAD VIII, held in Cartagena in 1992. At this water-shed meeting, the North successfully opposed all linkages of UNCTAD discussions with the Uruguay Round negotiations of the General Agreement on Tariffs and Trade (GATT) and man-aged to erode UNCTAD's negotiation functions, thus calling its existence into question. UNCTAD's main function would hence-forth be limited to "analysis, consensus building on some trade-related issues, and technical assistance."

This drastic curtailing of UNCTAD's scope was apparently not enough for certain northern interests. For instance, the Geneva-based Independent Commission on Global Governance identified UNCTAD as one of the agencies that could be abol-ished in order to streamline the UN system. The commission's views apparently coincided with that of Karl Theodor Paschke, head of the newly created UN Office of Internal Oversight

Services, who was quoted by *Stern* magazine as saying that UNCTAD had been made obsolete by the creation of the World Trade Organization (WTO). The truth of the matter is that although UNCTAD continues to survive, it has indeed been rendered impotent by the WTO, which replaced the less-powerful GATT following the conclusion of the eight-year Uruguay Round in 1994.

THE WORLD TRADE ORGANIZATION: SEALING THE DEFEAT OF THE SOUTH

THE WTO WAS NOT the first attempt at a global trading organization. Forty-six years previous, liberal internationalists had worked to create such an institution as a third pillar of the Bretton Woods system, but the threat of nonratification by unilateralist forces in the U.S. Senate led to its being shelved in favor of the much weaker GATT by the defensive Truman Administration.

By the mid-1980s, the United States became the lead advocate of a much-expanded GATT with real coercive teeth. U.S. officials were motivated by trade rivalries with Europe and Japan, the rising import penetration of the U.S. market by Third World countries, frustration at the inability of U.S. goods to enter southern markets, and the rise of new competitors in East Asia. Central to the founding of the WTO were the twin drives of managing the trade rivalry among the leading industrial countries and containing the threat posed by the South to the prevailing global economic structure. In this sense, the WTO must be seen as a continuation or extension of the same northern reaction that drove structural adjustment.

Indeed, the WTO, by enshrining the principle of free trade as the organizing principle of the global trading system, represents the defeat of everything that the South fought for in UNCTAD: fair prices via commodity price agreements; trade preferences to facilitate economic development in the South; preferential treatment for local investors; the use of trade policy as a legitimate instrument for industrialization; and a more concerted technology transfer to the South.

Instead, the WTO institutionalizes free trade, the most-favored nation principle, and national treatment as the pillars of the new world trading order. National treatment, established through the General Agreement on Trade in Services (GATS) of the Uruguay Round, is perhaps the most revolutionary and the most threatening to the South. This principle gives foreign service providers, from telecommunications companies to lawyers to educational agencies, the same rights and privileges as their domestic counterparts. Although the GATT-WTO Accord does recognize the "special and differential status" of the developing countries, it does not see this as a case of structurally determined differences but as one of gaps that can be surmounted by giving developing countries a longer adjustment period than the developed countries. While northern environmental organizations are critical of the WTO for subordinating northern environmental standards to the principle that Lori Wallach of Public Citizen describes as "free trade, uber alles," the southern countries have articulated their concerns about the GATT-WTO's antidevelopmental thrust. In their view, GATT-WTO is inherently unsympathetic to industrialization at the same time that it erodes the agricultural base of the developing societies.

A. THE WTO AND INDUSTRIALIZATION IN THE SOUTH

IN SIGNING ON TO GATT, Third World countries have agreed to ban all quantitative restrictions on imports, to reduce tariffs on many industrial imports, and not to raise tariffs on all other imports. In so doing, they have effectively given up the use of trade policy to pursue industrialization objectives. The way that the NICs made it to industrial status, via the policy of import substitution, is now effectively removed as a route to industrialization.

The anti-industrialization thrust of the GATT-WTO Accord is made even more manifest in the Agreement on Trade-Related Investment Measures (TRIMs) and the Agreement on Trade-Related Intellectual Property Rights (TRIPs). These agreements deny countries the right to pursue some of the policies that the NICs used successfully in their drive to industrialize. For example, countries like South Korea and Malaysia used trade-balancing requirements, which tied the value of a foreign investor's imports of raw materials and components to the value of his or her exports of the finished commodity, and "local content" regulations, which mandated that a certain percentage of the components that went into the making of a product be sourced locally.

These rules enabled the NICs to raise income from capital-intensive exports, develop support industries, and bring in technology, while still protecting local entrepreneurs' preferential access to the domestic market. In Malaysia, for instance, the strategic use of local content policy enabled them to build a "national car," in cooperation with Mitsubishi, that has now achieved about 80 percent local content and controls 70 percent of the Malaysian market. Thanks to the TRIMs accord, these mechanisms are now illegal.

Like TRIMs, the TRIPs regime is seen as an obstacle to the industrialization efforts of Third World countries. TRIPs provides a generalized minimum patent protection of 20 years; increases the duration of the protection for semiconductors or computer chips; institutes draconian border regulations against products judged to be violating intellectual property rights; and places the burden of proof on the presumed violator of process patents.

These requirements make it more difficult for developing countries to have the level of access to cutting-edge technologies that was enjoyed by the NICs and almost all late-industrializing countries. The United States industrialized, to a great extent, by using but paying very little for British manufacturing innovations, as did the Germans. Japan industrialized by liberally borrowing U.S. technological innovations, but barely compensating the Americans for this. And the Koreans industrialized by quite liberally copying U.S. and Japanese product and process technologies.

But what is "technological diffusion" from the perspective of the late industrializer is "piracy" from that of the industrial leader. The TRIPs regime takes the side of the latter and will make the process of industrialization by imitation much more difficult from now on. It represents what UNCTAD describes as "a premature strengthening of the intellectual property system...that favors monopolistically controlled innovation over broad-based diffusion."

Southern countries perceive TRIPs as a victory for the U.S. high-tech industry, which has long been lobbying for stronger controls over the diffusion of innovations. Innovation in the knowledge-intensive high-tech sector—in electronic software and hardware, biotechnology, lasers, optoelectronics, and liquid crystal technology, to name a few—has become the central determinant of economic power in our time. And when any company in the NICs and Third World wishes to innovate, say in chip design, software programming, or computer assembly, it necessarily has to integrate several patented designs and processes, most of them from U.S. electronic hardware and software giants like Microsoft, Intel, and Texas Instruments. As the Koreans have bitterly learned, exorbitant multiple royalty payments to what has been called the American "high-tech mafia" keeps one's profit margins very low while reducing incentives for local innovation. The likely outcome is for a southern manufacturer simply to pay royalties for a technology rather than to innovate, thus perpetuating the technological dependence on northern firms.

Thus, TRIPs enables the technological leader, in this case the United States, to greatly influence the pace of technological and industrial development in rival industrialized countries, the NICs, and the Third World.

B. TRIPs and Agriculture

TRIPs is also of concern because of the threat it poses to the very existence of agrarian communities. Because it strengthens considerably the system of private patenting of intellectual property, TRIPs has opened the way for the privatization of products developed from genetic processes or communal technological innovation in the South. As one analyst puts it, "Once modified, no matter how slightly, such genetic material can be patented by corporations or individuals who thus appropriate all financial benefits. As it stands now, an individual or company can collect a plant from a developing country, modify it or isolate a useful gene, and patent a new plant variety or product that contains it, without having to make any payment whatever to the communities whose traditional knowledge enabled the plant to be identified in the first place."

The GATT-WTO Accord does mention the possibility of a sui generis system for patenting agricultural products and process technologies, which could apply to those developed collectively by agrarian communities and indigenous peoples in the South. However, the emphasis of TRIPs is on the privatization of the nexus between natural processes and human intervention.

The threat posed by TRIPs to Third World agrarian communities is no longer one that is simply looming on the horizon. A U.S. firm has patented a new variety of seed produced from genetic material from jasmine rice developed in Thailand and basmati rice developed in India. Monsanto is now enforcing its proprietary rights to the use of seeds from harvests produced by "Monsanto-improved" seeds purchased by farmers. W.R. Grace has applied for and received a U.S. patent for the process extracting an active ingredient of the Neem tree, which is known for its wide variety of medical and other uses in India.

There are other, lesser known examples of what some scholars from the South have labeled "biopiracy" in the guise of intellectual property rights. One U.S. pharmaceutical company stands to make millions of dollars from two drugs, an anticarcinogenic and antileukemia agent, whose source is Madagascar. Merck, a leading Western pharmaceutical firm, is also likely to profit from the anticoagulant it is developing from the tikluba plant, which has long been used by indigenous peoples in the Amazon. Some eleven patents have already been filed in the United States and Japan covering the extraction and use of nata de coco from coconut, a major cottage industry in the Philippines, and patents by foreign entities and individuals are reported to have been filed on lagundi and banaba, two Philippine plants with medicinal qualities.

C. THE AGREEMENT ON AGRICULTURE

THE TRIPs ACCORD is an example of the double standards in the GATT-WTO. While it pushes free trade on the South in some of its subsidiary agreements, it actually promotes monopoly for the North in others. This is true as well of the Agreement on Agriculture (AOA), which will be opened up for new negotiations after the Third Ministerial in Seattle in late November 1999.

A close examination of the development and impact of the AOA would be useful for it illustrates how the trade superpowers' rivalry, which is one of the driving forces of the GATT-WTO, intersects with the equally dominant dynamic of subordinating the South to the North.

Prior to the Uruguay Round, agriculture was de facto outside GATT discipline, mainly because in the 1950s the United States had sought from GATT a waiver of Article XI, which prohibited quantitative restrictions on imports. With the United States threatening to leave GATT unless it was allowed to maintain protective mechanisms for sugar, dairy products, and other agricultural commodities, Washington was given a "non-time-limited waiver" on agricultural products. This led to the GATT's lax enforcement of Article XI on other agricultural producers for fear of being accused of having double standards.

The United States and the other agricultural powers not only ignored Article XI but they also exploited Article XVI, which exempted agricultural products from the GATT's ban on subsidies. One effect of these moves was the transformation of the European Union (EU) from being a net food importer into a net food exporter in the 1970s. By the beginning of the Uruguay Round in the mid-1980s, the EU's Common Agricultural Policy (CAP) had developed into what was described as "a complex web of price and sales guarantees, subsidies, and other support measures that largely insulated farmers' incomes from market forces."

With domestic prices set considerably above world prices and no controls on production, European farmers expanded production. The mounting surpluses could only be disposed of through exports, sparking competition with the previously dominant subsidized U.S. farmers for third-country markets. The competition between the agricultural superpowers turned fierce, but it was not so much their subsidized farmers who suffered. The victims were largely farmers in the South, such as the small-scale cattle growers of West Africa and South Africa, who were driven to ruin by low-priced EU exports of subsidized beef.

With state subsidies mounting to support the bitter competition for third-country markets, the EU and the United States gradually came to realize that continuing along the same path could only lead to a no-win situation for both. By the late 1980s, for instance, close to 80 percent of the EU's budget was going to support agricultural programs, and the United States had inaugurated a whole new set of expensive programs, such as the Export Enhancement Program, to win back markets, such as the North African wheat market, from the EU.

This mutual realization of the need for rules in the struggle for third-country markets is what led the EU and the United States to press for the inclusion of agriculture in the Uruguay Round. Rather than seriously promoting a mechanism to advance free trade, the two superpowers resorted to the rhetoric of free trade to regulate a condition of monopolistic competition, with each seeking advantage at the margins. The manner in which the AOA came into being lends support to this interpretation. The final agreement was essentially the Blair House Accord, which was only negotiated between the United States and the EU in 1992 and 1993. The Accord was then promptly relabeled the GATT Agreement on Agriculture and tossed to other GATT members by the two superpowers in 1994 on a take-it-or-leave-it basis. Understandably, many of the other GATT members, and not only those from the South, felt that they were practically coerced into signing the agreement.

The key provisions of the AOA are the following:

◆ Domestic support, quantified into a common measure called the "Aggregate Measure of Support," would be reduced by 20 percent over a six-year period; that is, AMS would be 20 percent lower in 2001 than AMS was in 1986–88. However, certain domestic subsidies, including direct income payments for farmers (the so-called "Green Box" and "Blue Box" measures) were exempted from cuts.

◆ Export subsidies would be reduced over a six-year period by 21 percent in volume and by 36 percent in terms of total cash value, and members would agree not to expand subsidies beyond the level reached at the end of the six-year period.

◆ Import quotas would be transformed into tariffs (tariffication), and these tariffs would be reduced over a period of six years by an average of 31 percent, with a 15 percent minimum tariff line, again with the base being the "tariff equivalents" of these quotas in 1986–88.

◆ Countries would pledge to allow a certain level of agricultural imports (minimum access volumes) that would start at three percent of 1986–88 consumption and rise to five percent in 1999.

◆ Under the so-called "special differential status" treatment accorded to them under GATT, developing countries would be subject to only two-thirds of the cuts in tariffs, domestic support, and export subsidies applied to developed countries, and they would be given a grace period of ten years, instead of six, to put these into effect.

By the time of the Seattle Ministerial in late 1999, the agreement will have been in effect for nearly five years, but, so far, it appears to have had little effect in terms of reducing the protection and subsidization enjoyed by agriculture in developed countries. Several mechanisms have worked to produce these results.

First, for the aggregate measure of support, export subsidies, and tariffs, the 1986–88 levels at which the items were bound were quite high relative to the levels in 1995 when the AOA took effect, resulting in minimal actual reductions in subsidies and tariffs. In fact, the United States was able under these guidelines to raise its simple average tariffs significantly between 1992 and 1996 (from 5.7 percent to 8.5 percent for agriculture and livestock production, from 6.6 percent to 10.0 percent for food products, and from 14.6 to 104.4 percent for tobacco products). Also, the Uruguay Round's requirements that import quotas be transformed into tariffs has been abused by the EU and the United States, with the latter, for instance, levying an ad valorem duty of 350 percent for above-minimum-access imports of tobacco products.

Second, the rules for achieving the 36 percent average tariff reduction were quite loose. Countries could meet them through a combination of minimal tariff cuts on sensitive or valued product lines and deep cuts on nonsensitive products, and by "backloading" their already minimal tariff cuts on the valued products toward the end of the six-year period.

Third, subsidies such as direct income payments to make up for the vagaries of the market have been exempted from cuts. Such payments were excluded on the specious grounds that they were "decoupled from production" and thus "nontrade distorting." This loophole primarily benefits farmers in rich countries, which can afford to make such direct payments. This exemption was a major blow to the hopes of many countries that the AOA would serve as a mechanism for leveling the playing field between farmers in the North and South.

In the EU, these direct income payments are mainly based on output, the bulk of them via a "land set-aside program" that entitles each farmer to a subsidy when she or he withdraws 15 percent of his/her land from cultivation. The idea behind the set-aside program is to restrict output, thus raising prices. In the U.S. Farm Bill, farmers get the same level of direct income subsidy in good and bad crop years. Deficiency payments are projected to average US$5.1 billion a year between 1996 and 2002.

But the truth is that direct payments to European and U.S. farmers are anything but decoupled from production, since without them agriculture would scarcely remain profitable. Deficiency payments, for instance, make up between one-fifth and one-third of U.S. farm incomes. In other words, in enshrining the notion of decoupled payments as untouchable subsidies in Green Box, the United States and the EU were, as one analyst put it, "taking away direct support of markets and replacing it with direct subsidization of [northern] farmers." The combination of minimal cuts in tariffs, export subsidies, and AMS, and the maintenance of direct income payments has had the predictable result of raising the total amount of agricultural subsidies in the OECD countries since the Agreement came into force: from US$182 billion in 1995 to an astounding $280 billion in 1997, with the major share of this figure accounted for by the EU and the United States. More than 40 percent of the total value of production in the OECD countries is now accounted for by different forms of producer subsidies.

In contrast to this massive subsidization in the OECD countries, farmers in many developing countries have experienced low and declining government financial support. Where subsidization does exist, it often does not even reach the level allowed by the AOA, set at 10 percent of the value of production. In fact, developing countries have been penalized by policies that have brought about the "negative subsidization" of their agricultural sector. Yet it is the farmers of these countries of the South that will be forced to bear the burden of adjustment to the new agricultural regime, because their lack of subsidies is paralleled by their clear commitment to give greater market access to northern farming interests, whose runaway subsidization continues to push them to create mountains of commodities seeking export outlets.

A 1997 report to the EU farm ministers projected the surplus of wheat to rise from 2.7 million metric tons to 45 million tons by 2005 and the total cereal surplus to shoot up to 58 million metric tons. The solution to this condition of subsidized overproduction, said EU Agriculture Minster Franz Fischler, was intensified efforts to export grain. Continuing subsidization has also deepened U.S. agriculture's dependence on massive exporting. Admitting that "one out of every three farm acres in America is dedicated to exports," USTR Charlene Barshefky has concluded that "given the limitations inherent in U.S. demand-led growth, we must find new markets for American agriculture. We must open new markets to support the increasingly productive U.S. agricultural sector."

So the story continues: subsidized Northern producers that make a mockery of global free trade in agriculture fight for developing country markets, squeezing the nonsubsidized farmers in the latter.

Undoubtedly, the AOA does offer some concessions to the South in the form of the lifting of quotas and some reduction in tariffs on developing country exports of commercial crops like palm oil and coconut oil. But these are concessions that benefit mainly organized lobbies of cash-crop exporters and processors, such as Malaysian palm-oil plantations, big cocoa and coffee planters in Africa and Asia, and big sugar interests in the Caribbean. The vast majority of unorganized small farmers specializing in corn, rice, and other food crops are hurt by this trade-off, for the quid pro quo is precisely the liberalization of their markets for staples and other basic foods.

In the case of Southeast Asia, for instance, limited gains for palm-oil interests in Malaysia and coconut-oil exporters in Manila stemming from the Uruguay Round have been outbalanced by the tremendous damage imposed by liberalization on rice farmers in Malaysia, Indonesia, and the Philippines. Thai rice farmers are hardly benefiting; it's the Bangkok-based middlemen who are profiting from increased Thai rice exports. Further liberalization in a new round of negotiations will simply drive the region's small farmers over the edge, as it will the small farmers in other parts of the South.

Perhaps the profound inequality institutionalized in the AOA was best summed up by the Philippines' Secretary of Trade and Industry in his speech at the Second Ministerial of the WTO in May 1998: "The Agriculture Agreement as it now stands ...has perpetuated the unevenness of the playing field which the multi-lateral trading system has been seeking to correct. Moreover, this has placed the burden of adjustment on developing countries relative to countries who can afford to maintain high levels of domestic support and export subsidies."

D. OLIGARCHIC DECISION MAKING

THERE ARE OTHER INEQUALITIES structured into the WTO system. The system of decision making is perhaps among the most blatant of these. Pro-WTO propaganda has projected the agency as a "one nation/one vote" organization, where the United States has no more votes than Rwanda or the Dominican Republic. In fact, it is quite undemocratic and is actually run by an oligarchy of countries, much like the World Bank and the IMF. Were majority rule to prevail, then the WTO would, like the UN General Assembly, be structurally more responsive to the needs of the South. But, as it did at the World Bank and the IMF, the North evolved other mechanisms of control. While at the Bank and the Fund the prime mechanism of control is the size of rich countries' financial contributions, which gives them enormous voting power vis-a-vis the mass of developing countries, at the WTO, northern domination is achieved via what is euphemistically referred to as "consensus."

This process was described in the following manner before the U.S. Congress by an influential WTO advocate: after noting that there had not been a vote taken in GATT, the WTO's predecessor, since 1959, economist C. Fred Bergsten underlined that the WTO "does not work by voting. It works by a consensus arrangement which, to tell the truth, is managed by four—the Quads: the United States, Japan, European Union, and Canada." He continued: "Those countries have to agree if any major steps

are going to be made, that is true. But no votes. I do not antici-
pate votes in the new institution."

The way that the consensus rule assures the hegemony of
the North was recently on display in the selection of the successor to Renato Ruggiero as director general. The U.S.-led bloc
that successfully supported New Zealander Mike Moore refused
a head count, as proposed by backers of Thailand's Supachai, on
grounds that this would violate the WTO's consensus tradition.

Indeed, so undemocratic is the WTO that decisions are
arrived at informally, via caucuses convoked in the corridors of
the ministerials by the big trading powers. The formal sessions
are reserved for speeches. The key agreements to come out of
the first and second ministerials of the WTO—the decision to
liberalize information technology trade taken in Singapore in
1996 and the agreement to liberalize trade in electronic commerce arrived at in Geneva in 1998—were decided on in
informal backroom sessions and simply presented to the full
assembly as faits accomplis. It is against this dismal background
that we now move to the question of reform.

STRATEGY FOR CHANGE

AFTER INDICTING the Bretton Woods institutions, some people
turn around and appeal to these same institutions (and the
WTO) to become answerable to the UN and to reorient their
policies to serve the interests of the world's poor majority, arguing that this would be "truly in the enlightened self-interest of
people in the rich, industrialized countries, their children, and
their children's children."

This is utopian thinking, especially at a time that the North
has just completed a campaign of global rollback that has delivered the coup de grace to the southern project of reform. For

reform, not revolution, was what the NIEO, the Non-Aligned Movement, and UNCTAD were all about...and look where this already very limited enterprise—what one northern observer described as "the present order, with extra helpings for the flag bearers of the South"—got the Third World. Change at this time means not wasting time trying to enlarge areas of reform within the World Bank, IMF, and WTO. These are, to borrow a metaphor from Max Weber, an iron cage of three overlapping bureaucracies and mandates where southern aspirations and interests are structurally constrained.

One prong of a possible counter-strategy for defending the interests of the South must be directed at preserving the legitimacy of the UN system, at a time when its effectiveness as an instrument of development is hobbled by northern hostility and a lack of money. That a little money can go a long way, when funneled into the right instrument, is shown by the example of the UNDP Human Development Report, which is now seen as the magisterial authority in both the North and the South on the social and economic state of the world, no matter what the whole arsenal of World Bank publications says. A good candidate for doing in trade what the Human Development Report does for development is the UNCTAD Trade and Development Report, whose focus on global structures impeding the ascent of the South is a good antidote to the WTO publications' doctrinal assertions on the benefits of free trade.

Beyond this, however, the project of making the UN agencies the pillars of an alternative global order is not going to result in success for a long, long time. What, then, should southern movements for global reform focus their energies on? The main thrust, in our view, is to overload the system, to make it non-functional by constantly pushing demands that cannot be met by the system. For instance, in the case of the IMF, governments of the South and NGO's can press for the following demands:

- more transparency in IMF decision making
- more accountability of IMF staff
- one country/one vote decision making arrangements
- an end to structural adjustment programs
- no new funding for extended structural adjustment programs (ESAF)
- no extension of IMF authority to governance issues and
- subordination of structural adjustment programs to global environmental agreements

When it comes to the WTO, among the key tactics that could be deployed to overload the system might be:

- pressing for the replacement of consensus decision making with majority voting
- the creative use of antidumping mechanisms against import penetration and
- exploiting loopholes in the Sanitary and Phyto-sanitary Agreement to restrict agricultural imports

Developing country governments must approach WTO rules in the same way that a good defense lawyer approaches criminal law, which is to exploit the ambiguities of the system for the sake of the client—in this case for Third World farmers, manufacturers, and other producers.

Of course, the success of a strategy of overloading the system depends greatly on creating global political alliances, including coalitions with antiglobalization social and political forces in the North. There are examples to draw from: A global pressure campaign by NGOs from both the North and the South on OECD governments prevented the adoption of the Multilateral Agreement on Investment (MAI) by that body. NGO pressure on the U.S. Congress killed the granting of "fast-track" authority to negotiate free-trade agreements to the U.S. president, weakening the ability of the United States to demand greater trade liberalization at the Seattle WTO Ministerial.

Where structures are hopeless, the next best solution is to have nonfunctioning structures or no operative structures at all. It was, for instance, during a period where no bodies supervised aid and development—the World War II era and immediate postwar era—that the countries of Latin America were able to successfully engage in import substitution to build up industrial structures. And it was during the period from the 1960s up to the late 1980s, before the establishment of the WTO, that the NICs of East and Southeast Asia were able to marry domestic protectionism to mercantilism to move from underdevelopment to industrial status in one generation.

Multilateral structures entrench the power of the northern superpowers under the guise of creating a set of global rules for all. This is the reason why, in promoting the WTO in the U.S. Congress, former USTR Mickey Kantor characterized the WTO as a "sword" that can be used to pry open economies. This is the reason Washington's academic point man on trade, C. Fred Bergsten, could tell the U.S. Senate that ratification of the Uruguay Round would serve the interests of the United States because in addition to unilateral action, "we can now use the full weight of the international machinery to go after those trade barriers, reduce them, get them eliminated."

Though the threat of unilateral action by the powerful is ever present, on balance a global system where there are either no multilateral structures or ineffective ones works to the benefit of the South.

Of course, the ideologues of the North will shout that this is tantamount to "anarchy." But then it has always been the powerful that have stoked this fear. The image of international relations in a world marked by few international arrangements as "nasty" and "brutish" has always been a Hobbesian fallacy that has not corresponded to reality. For the principal objective of most multilateral or international arrangements in history has never been to assure law and order to protect the weak. These structures have been pushed by the strong, mainly to reduce the tremendous cost of policing the system to ensure that the less powerful will not cease to respect the rules set by the more powerful or break away completely.

In short, a fluid international system, where there are multiple zones of ambiguity that the less powerful can exploit in order to protect their interests, may be the only realistic alternative to the current global multilateral order that would weaken the hold of the North. The main beneficiaries of clearly articulated structures are always the powerful and the rich. The fewer structures and the less clear the rules, the better for the South.

WAR AGAINST NATURE AND THE PEOPLE OF THE SOUTH

Dr. Vandana Shiva

Vandana Shiva is a physicist, founder and president of the Research Foundation for Science Technology and Ecology, and one of India's leading activists. She played a key role in the famous Chipko movement to save the Himalayan forests and now works on behalf of India's farmers, trying to resist the introduction of globalized industrial agriculture and biotechnology into Indian food production. She is a member of the Board of Directors of the International Forum on Globalization, and was a recipient of the Right Livelihood Award (also known as the alternative Nobel Peace Prize). Her most recent book is Biopiracy: The Plunder of Nature and Knowledge *(Boston: South End Press, 1997).*

In this paper, Shiva describes how the transformation of peasant agriculture in India to a globally industrialized model has reduced food security, threatened local businesses and biodiversity, driven farmers off their lands, and opened the door for global corporations to take over the nation's food processing. Shiva then examines the forces driving the globalization of agriculture, including the agribusiness giants and two of the WTO agreements these firms have promoted: the agreements on agriculture and intellectual property rights.

SUPPORTERS OF GLOBALIZATION often claim that this process is natural, inevitable, and evolutionary and one that is bringing prosperity and growth, embracing us all and knitting us into a Global Village. Only by participating in global markets, they say, can Third World people get access to jobs and better lives. In reality, globalization is not a natural process of inclusion. It is a planned project of exclusion that siphons the resources and knowledge of the poor of the South into the global marketplace, stripping people of their life-support systems, livelihoods, and lifestyles.

Global trade rules, as enshrined in the World Trade Organization (WTO) Agreement on Agriculture (AOA) and in the Trade Related Intellectual Property Rights (TRIPs) agreement, are primarily rules of robbery, camouflaged by arithmetic and legalese. In this economic hijack, the corporations gain, and people and nature loose.

The WTO's overall goal of promoting "market competition" serves two functions. Firstly, it transforms all aspects of life into commodities for sale. Culture, biodiversity, food, water, livelihoods, needs, and rights are all transformed and reduced to markets. Secondly, the destruction of nature, culture, and livelihoods is then justified on the basis of the rules of competition. Policy makers attack ethical and ecological rules that sustain and maintain life, claiming that they are "protectionist" barriers to trade. In reality, the WTO does not reduce protectionism; it merely replaces protections for people and nature with protections for corporations.

The global reach of corporations to take over the resources of the poor of the Third World is made possible not just by reduction and removal of tariffs, one of the goals of the WTO. It is facilitated by the removal of ethical and ecological limits on what can be owned as private property and what can be traded. In this way, globalization is completing the project of colonization that led to the conquest and ownership of land and territory. Biological resources and water, the very basis of life's processes, are being colonized, privatized, and commodified.

Agriculture, which is still the primary livelihood for three-quarters of humanity, and which is as much a cultural activity as an economic one, is also threatened by "trade liberalization," driven both by the structural adjustment programs of the World Bank and the IMF, and by the WTO's Agreement on Agriculture.[1] The globalization of food and agriculture systems, in effect, means the corporate takeover of the food chain, the erosion of food rights, the destruction of the cultural diversity of food and the biological diversity of crops, and the displacement of millions from land-based, rural livelihoods. Global free trade in food and agriculture is the biggest refugee creation program in the world, far exceeding the impact of Kosovo. It is equivalent to the ethnic cleansing of the poor, the peasantry, and small farmers of the Third World.

GLOBALIZATION OF INDIA'S AGRICULTURE

TRADE AND INVESTMENT LIBERALIZATION have led to a dramatic transformation of agriculture in India that has had a devastating impact on peasant farmers. These policies have brought about:

- ◆ a shift in production from food to export crops that has reduced food security
- ◆ a flood of imports that have wiped out local businesses and diversity and
- ◆ an opening for global corporations to take over the control of food processing.

A. Shift to Export Crops
Cotton: Seeds of Suicide

Economic globalization is leading to a concentration of the seed industry, the entry of global corporations into agriculture, the increased use of pesticides, and, finally, increased debt, despair, and sometimes suicide among small farmers. Capital-intensive, corporate-controlled agriculture is being spread into regions where peasants are poor but, until now, have been self-sufficient in food. In the regions where industrial agriculture has been introduced through globalization, higher costs are making it virtually impossible for small farmers to survive.

The new export-oriented policies that are part of agricultural globalization have led to a shift in India from the production of food crops to commodities for exports, such as cotton. Cotton cultivation has expanded even into semiarid areas such as Warangal in Andhra Pradesh, where farmers traditionally grew paddy, pulses, millets, oilseeds, and vegetable crops. Enticed by promises that cotton would be like "white gold," yielding high profits, farmers in Warangal have nearly tripled the amount of land used for cotton production in the past decade, while slashing production of traditional food grains like jawar and bajra.

However, what these farmers have learned is that while cash crops like cotton may fetch higher prices, they also demand a higher level of expenditure. Under corporate pressure, farmers have largely switched from planting open-pollinated seeds, which can be saved by farmers, to hybrids that need to be purchased every year at a high cost. Because hybrids are very vulnerable to pest attacks, pesticide use has also increased. Expenditures on pesticide in the district went up from $2.5 million for the entire decade of the 1980s to $50 million in 1997—a 2,000 percent increase. For poor peasants, this cost could be borne only through debts.[2]

Because trade liberalization had also led to budget cutbacks

on extension and withdrawal of low-interest credit from cooper-
atives and public sector banks, peasants have had to take
high-interest loans from the same companies that sell them
hybrid seeds and pesticides. Thus, the corporations have become
money lenders, extension agents, seed suppliers, and pesticide
salesmen rolled into one. As a result, peasants have become
buried under the weight of unpayable debt. This financial stress
is blamed for an epidemic of suicides in Warangal district. More
than 500 farmers took their own lives in 1998, and the suicides
have continued in 1999.

In the regions where high costs of industrial agriculture
introduced through globalization are already pushing farmers to
suicide, Monsanto has tried to introduce genetically engineered
cotton seeds. While the argument used to promote these crops
in the Third World is that they will increase yields, trials have
shown a decrease in yields and an increase in the use of pesticides.[3] In protest, farmers in Andhra Pradesh and Karnataka have
uprooted the genetically engineered cotton, and the Research
Foundation for Science, Technology, and Ecology has filed a case
in the Supreme Court to stop the introduction of these genetically
engineered crops in Indian agriculture.[4] The case is based on the
belief that genetic engineering would introduce new ecological
and economic risks that Third World peasants cannot afford.[5]

Shrimp Factories
The shift from a "food first" to an "export first" policy is justified
on grounds of food security, because export earnings are supposed
to pay for food imports. In fact, export-oriented agriculture has
reduced food security by encouraging a shift from small-scale,
sustainable production to large-scale, non-sustainable industrial
production. It also brings changes in ownership over natural
resources and means of production, from small autonomous pro-
ducer/owners to large corporate and commercial interests. Peasants

are displaced from farming, while commercial interests take over land for industrial-scale production of export commodities such as shrimp, flowers, vegetables, and meat. These enterprises often have negative environmental impacts, creating further hardship for local communities.

The transformation of shrimp farming in India is a prime example of the social and environmental costs of industrial agriculture. While small-scale, indigenous shrimp farming has been sustainable over centuries, shrimp exports require the establishment of factory farms for shrimp production. Each acre of a shrimp farm needs 200 "shadow acres" for absorbing the ecological costs of factory farming of shrimp. "Shadow acres" are the units required to supply resources to and absorb the waste from a particular economic activity.

Shrimp farming is so damaging because it requires enormous quantities of fish to be caught at sea for shrimp feed, most of which is converted to waste that is poured into the sea, polluting the water and damaging mangroves. Shrimp farming also destroys coastal agriculture because the shrimp factories require the pumping of seawater into the ponds for shrimp production. This causes salinization, reducing drinking water supplies and destroying trees and crops near the factories.

These costs undermine the claims that shrimp exports are a major source of economic growth. For each dollar earned by corporations through exports of shrimp to consumers in the United States, Europe, and Japan, an estimated $10 worth of damage is done to India's natural resources and local economic income. This includes the destruction of mangroves, water, agriculture, and fisheries.[6]

Shrimp factories have met with stiff resistance in India. In December 1996, local communities and environmental groups won a case in the Indian Supreme Court to ban industrial shrimp farming. However, the shrimp industry received a stay order, and continues to operate.[7] On May 29, 1999, four fishermen were killed when they protested against the commercial shrimp operators called the "shrimp mafia" in the Chilka lake in Orissa.

This tragedy illustrates how the inequalities aggravated or generated by export-oriented agriculture can also lead to violations of human rights and subversion of law and order. Trade can only be increased by taking resources away from people's subsistence and survival. When people attempt to defend their human right to work and live, commercial interests that gain from exports often work with the state apparatus to crush people's movements. Many people lose what little they have. In the most extreme cases, such as that of the Orissa fishermen, they pay for exports with their lives.

Other Export Crops: Costs Exceed Earnings
Like shrimp exports, flower, meat, and vegetable exports have costs that often far exceed the earnings generated. Large scale meat exports, for example, have an external "shadow" cost that is ten times higher than export earnings. This is due to the former ecological contribution of livestock in small-scale agriculture, now on the wane.

Particularly in developing countries, livestock are not just meat on legs. Animals are the primary source of fertilizer in the form of organic manure. They also generate energy for farm operations, by plowing, and by helping with agro-processing; for example, with edible oil extraction via animal-driven "ghanis." Livestock in India help produce $17 million worth of milk, and $1.5 billion worth of food grain; they also provide $17 million worth of energy.[8] If the animals are slaughtered, all of these benefits are lost. In the case of one export-oriented slaughterhouse alone, meat exports earned $45 million, whereas the estimated contribution of the slaughtered animals to the economy if they had been allowed to live was $230 million.[9]

In the case of flowers, countries must import plant material, pesticides, greenhouse equipment and pay for consultants. India spent Rs. 13.7 billion in foreign exchange to import inputs for floriculture and earned only Rs. 0.3 billion from flower sales, thus having a net drain of Rs. 10 billion on scarce foreign change.[10]

If the resources used for floriculture had been allocated for food production, India would have produced four times more food than it could buy on global markets using earnings from flower sales. In terms of national food security, export-oriented agriculture therefore destroys more than it creates.

Under the pressure of so-called "liberalization" policies, food prices have doubled and the poor have had to cut their consumption in half. Prices have increased because food has been exported, creating domestic scarcity, at the same time that food subsidies have been withdrawn. As a housewife in Bombay stated "we are eating half of what we used to after food prices doubled in the last year. Even dal is a luxury now. After milk prices increased, I stopped buying milk as well." [11]

Export-oriented agriculture is also creating an agricultural apartheid, with the Third World being asked to stop growing food staples and instead grow luxury products for the rich North. Production of food staples is now concentrated in the United States, and in the hands of a few multinational seed companies and grain trading companies.

B. IMPORTS: DIVERSITY DESTROYED

AS COUNTRIES ARE FORCED to destroy their agricultural systems to grow and export commodities, both cultural diversity and biological diversity disappear. Diverse cereals, oilseeds, and legumes are displaced by soybeans from the United States. While exports destroy local food systems by diverting resources and changing ownership patterns, imports also destroy food systems by hijacking markets.

In August 1999, there was a case of mustard oil adulteration that was restricted to the city of Delhi, but affected all local brands of oil. In response, the government banned mustard oil, the main cooking oil in North India, and removed all restrictions on edible oil imports.[12] Soybean and soy oil imports were liberalized or deregulated. Within one growing season, millions of oilseed-producing farmers growing mustard, groundnut, sesame, and niger had lost the market for their diverse oil seed crops. Liberalized imports of soybeans have destroyed the entire edible oil production and processing in India. Millions of small mills have closed down. Prices of oilseeds have collapsed and farmers cannot even recover what they have spent on cultivation. Sesame, linseed, and mustard have started to disappear from the fields as cheap, subsidized imports of soybeans are dumped on the Indian market. These imports totaled three million tons in one year (a 60 percent rise compared to earlier years) and cost nearly $1 billion, thus worsening the country's balance of payments situation.[13]

U.S. soybeans are cheap not because of cheap production but because of subsidies. The price of soybeans is $155 a ton, and this low price is possible because the U.S. government pays $193 a ton to U.S. soybean farmers, who would not otherwise be able to stay in production given the low commodity prices. This government support is not really a farmer subsidy; it is an indirect corporate subsidy. As heavily subsidized soybeans flooded India's domestic market, prices crashed by more than two thirds. The local oil processing industry, from the small-scale "ghanis" to larger mills, started to close down. Domestic oilseed production declined, and domestic edible oil prices crashed. Groundnut prices went down by 3 percent from Rs. 48 per kilogram to Rs. 37 per kilogram. Meanwhile, some farmers protesting against the collapse of their markets were shot and killed.

C. CORPORATE CONTROL OF PROCESSING AND PACKAGING

GLOBAL AGRIBUSINESS is now attempting to take over food processing by making fresh, locally produced food appear backward, and stale food clothed in aluminum and plastic appear "modern." Industrial processing and packaging was first applied to edible oils, destroying the livelihoods of millions of oil mill operators and small farmers because of imported soybeans. An attempt is now being made to take over the wheat economy.

Wheat is called *"kanak,"* the word for gold in North India. The Indian wheat economy is based on decentralized, small-scale local production, processing, and distribution systems. Wheat and flour *(atta)* provide livelihoods and nutrition to millions of farmers, traders *(artis)*, and local mill operators *(chakki wallas)*.

The decentralized, small-scale, household-based economy of food production and processing is huge in aggregate. It generates millions of livelihoods while ensuring that fresh and wholesome food at accessible prices is available to people. Moreover, such production and processing has no negative environmental impacts.

Millions of Indian farmers grow 6,050 million tons of wheat every year.[14] Most of this is bought as wheat by consumers from the local corner store *(kirana)* and taken to the local *chakki walla*. A chain of *artis*, or traders, bring the wheat from the farm to the local shops.

It is estimated that more than 3.5 million family-run *kirana* shops supply wheat to Indian consumers. More than 2 million small neighborhood mills produce fresh flour. In addition, flour is also produced by millions of women working at the household level. The rolling pin *(belan)* used for making *"rotis"* has always been a symbol of women's power. It is often mistakenly said that only 2 percent of food is processed in India. This is because officials ignore women's work in the home and the contribution of this work to the national economy.

While 40 million tons of wheat is traded, only 15 million tons is purchased directly as *atta* because Indians love freshness and quality in food. Less than 1 percent of the consumed *atta* carries a brand name because Indian consumers trust their own supervision of quality at the local *chakki* better than a brand name attached to stale, packaged flour.

This decentralized, small-scale economy based on millions of producers, processors and traders works with very little capital and very little infrastructure. People are the substitute for capital and infrastructure. However, such a people-centered economy impedes large-scale profits for big agribusiness. They are therefore eyeing the Indian wheat economy to transform it into a source of profits.

In an industry report entitled *"Faida"* (profit), the hijack of the wheat and atta supply by global agribusiness is described as the "wheat opportunity in India." Their plan is based on making farmers directly dependent on agribusiness corporations for purchase of inputs such as seeds, destroying local seed supply, and displacing the local *artis* or traders and destroying the local *chakki wallas*.

The destruction of millions of livelihoods, of the local decentralized economy, and of people's access to fresh and cheap *atta*, is described as "modernization of the food chain." In the Third World, packaged food is described as the food of the rich, even though the rich in industrialized countries in fact eat fresh food, while the poor are forced to eat heavily processed and packaged food.

Packaging is not "modernization," but rather an obsolete aspect of a non-sustainable economy that uses packaging and brand names as a way to displace the more efficient and cheaper system through which people can get food processed locally in front of their eyes and hence ensure quality and freshness.

❖ ❖ ❖

India's wheat and *atta* economy is complex and highly developed, but global agribusiness defines it as underdeveloped because the big players like Cargill and Archer Daniels Midland (ADM) do not control it. As the *Faida* report states, "The Indian wheat sector is currently at a nascent stage of development. Despite its importance, the industry is at a very early stage of improvement."

The main criterion used to declare India's wheat economy underdeveloped is that the global corporations are missing from the scene. Underdevelopment is the absence of corporate control. "Development" is then defined as equivalent to the corporate hijack of the economy.

A decentralized, locally controlled, and small-scale system is defined as "nascent" and "underdeveloped," while monopolized food systems are defined as "developed." The hijack of the food system is thus made to appear as the "natural evolution" from small to big. Freshness and wholesomeness are defined as "low technology." Impure, stale flour with a brand name is defined as "high quality." This distorted attitude is reflected in a section of the *Faida* report that states, "As a result of the inadequate technology used by the millers, the shelf life of flour in India is typically 15 to 20 days. This is very short when compared to the six months to a year achieved in the United States." What the report fails to recognize is that the brand name players have no choice but to ensure a longer shelf life, given the huge distances between the factory and the markets.

The highest level of Orwellian doublespeak is being used to accomplish the hijack of wheat from Indian farmers and processors. Decentralization is defined as *fragmentation*. But *centralization* is defined as *integration*, even though decentralized, locally controlled systems are highly integrated while centrally controlled systems are based on disintegration of ecosystems and local economic communities.

Agribusiness has already started to try to get Indian consumers to doubt their own quality control systems and trust the brand names. They see a potential corporate-controlled market that would generate RS. 3,000 *crore* or RS. 10 billion of profits through sale of packaged, brand name wheat. The corporate agenda for India is to introduce monopolies in wheat such as those of Cargill and ADM, and in seed such as those of Monsanto, Novartis, Dupont, and Zeneca. These seed corporations demand monopolistic intellectual property rights to seed, forcing farmers to pay royalties while also controlling other inputs. This trend is moving the country toward an agricultural economy in which only a small number of people are involved—and only as tractor drivers and pesticide sprayers. All other functions of farmers—as maintainers of biodiversity, stewards of soil and water, and seed breeders—are destroyed.

The *Faida* report claims that 5 million jobs will be "created" by the takeover of the food chain by global corporations. However, it is well known that giant firms often invest in technology that is used to displace people. For example, ADM owns 200 grain elevators, 1,900 barges, 800 trucks, and 130,000 railcars to transport and store wheat. The number of jobs generated by ADM is not significant, however, because the company uses pneumatic blowers to load and unload grain and other technologies to lower labor costs.

Moreover, if one takes into account the 20-30 million farmers, 5 million *chakki wallas*, 5 million *artis*, 3.5 million *kirana* shops, and the households dependent on them, at least 100 million people's livelihoods and sustenance will be destroyed by the industrialization of the wheat economy alone.

THE DRIVING FORCES BEHIND
GLOBALIZATION OF AGRICULTURE

A. The Agribusiness Giants

Agribusiness giants have driven the process of globalization in their efforts to gain control over the world's agricultural economy, from selling seeds and other inputs, to trading commodities, to processing food.

One of the most ominous developments in the past decade has been the merger of chemical, pharmaceutical, biotechnology and seed companies to create what they call "Life Sciences" corporations. A more accurate name would be "Death Sciences" corporations because they produce genetically engineered, herbicide-tolerant seeds that lock farmers into dependence on chemical inputs, destroy biodiversity, and render agriculture more vulnerable. These corporations are also genetically engineering sterile seed, through what is called "Terminator Technology," so that farmers cannot save seed and are forced to buy seed every year.[15]

Monsanto is the world's largest biotechnology corporation. It controls large parts of the soybean and cotton seed supply through patents and through having acquired seed companies across the world, including Dekalb, Agracetus, Asgrow, Calgene, Holden, Delta and Pine Land, MAHYCO, Rallis, and the seed division of Cargill.

Commodities trading is also highly concentrated and becoming more so. U.S.-based Cargill, already the world's largest grain trader, recently merged with the second largest grain trading corporation, Continental Grain. Cargill also processes and distributes agricultural, food, financial, and industrial products and has approximately 80,600 employees in more than 1,000 locations in 65 countries and business activities in 130 more. Cargill controls over 70 percent of the world's trade in cereals.

Cargill's presence in India is also extensive. In 1998, Cargill became the biggest exporter of protein meal from India—having exported 300,000 tons. It also exported 10,000 tons of non-basmati rice. During 1999, it has procured 10,000 tons of wheat. It has entered into an agreement with the Punjab Government to procure wheat and rice, develop grain handling and storage facilities, and enter into contract farming of wheat. It already has its own pier in Jamnagar.

B. THE WTO AGREEMENT ON AGRICULTURE

ALL OVER THE WORLD, structural adjustment and trade liberalization have already driven millions of farmers off the land because of rising costs of production and collapsing prices of commodities. Instead of supporting policies that help farmers survive, WTO rules are driving small farmers to extinction and ensuring that agriculture is controlled by global corporations.

The Agreement on Agriculture (AOA) of the WTO is a rule-based system for trade liberalization of agriculture that was pushed by the United States in the Uruguay Round of the GATT. However, these rules are the wrong rules for protecting food security, nature, and culture. Instead, they are perfectly shaped for the objective of corporate rule over our food and agriculture systems.

The AOA rules apply to countries, even though it is not countries or their farmers that engage in global trade in agriculture but global corporations like Cargill. These firms gain from every rule that marginalizes farmers by removing support from agriculture. They gain from every rule that deregulates international trade, liberalizes exports and imports, and makes restrictions of exports and imports illegal. Market openings through the AOA are therefore market openings for the Cargills and Monsantos.

The outcome of negotiations for the AOA should not be surprising, because global agribusiness corporations held tremendous influence over the negotiations. In fact, the U.S. delegation was led by Clayton Yeutter, a former Cargill employee.

There are three components to the AOA:

◆ Domestic Support
◆ Market Access
◆ Export Competition

Domestic Support

The WTO clauses on "Domestic Support" demand commitment to reduce domestic "support" to producers by 20 percent of the country's 1986-1988 level by 1999. For developing countries, this has been reduced to 13 percent to be implemented over ten years.

Support is defined by a formula called the Aggregate Measure of Support (AMS). The AMS calculates all domestic support policies that are considered to have a significant effect on the volume of production. The AMS is nothing more than a device to anesthetize the public so that no one senses the hihack of food systems by corporate power. Through an extremely complicated and confusing system of "amber box," "green box," and "blue box" labeling, the WTO regime makes it difficult for citizens, policy makers, and governments to figure out what is really happening. Policies that do have a substantial impact on the patterns and flow of trade are classified as the "amber box" policies and are subject to reduction. These include budgetary outlays, foregone revenue, and payments at national and sub-national levels. Policies that are not deemed to have a major effect on production and trade are classified as the "green box." Policies that fall in between are called the "blue box."

There is a false assumption that these rules on Domestic Support will reduce subsidies for industrial agriculture and global trade, making small farmers and the Third World more competitive and leading to prices that reflect the true cost of production. This is not true for a number of reasons. The articles on Domestic Support target only a small fraction of subsidies in agriculture. For example, reduction of the "amber box" policies under AMS directly affects farmers, because these only address prices at the first point of sale. Additional subsidies enjoyed by global agribusiness and trading interests, such as subsidies for investment, fertilizer, marketing, and infrastructure, are all exempted. Thus, WTO rules allow support for corporations but not for farmers.

Other examples of how corporate, industrialized agriculture is given advantages through this box system are as follows:

◆　The allowable "green box" policies include "producer retirement" programs, "resource (land) retirement programs," environmental programs, marketing information, and infrastructure. The subsidy for producer retirement must be conditional on total and permanent retirement of the recipients from marketable agriculture production. Thus, farmers can get assistance to leave farming, but not for staying active as producers. The farmers also have no say in what happens to the land they leave. The subsidy for resource retirement must be conditional on retiring land from marketable agricultural production for at least three years, and in the case of livestock, on its slaughter or permanent disposal. For the most part, these "green box" policies will affect only farmers in affluent countries, since these governments are more able to pay for them.

◆　"Blue box" policies can include measures such as direct payments to farmers and land set-aside. These policies are allowed as long as the supports are "de-coupled" from production supports. This implies that direct payments can be provided to support incomes of farmers, and that the overall cost of production will not be reflected in the price of commodities. In effect, these exclusions imply that incomes of farmers in industrialized countries will be directly paid by governments, and will not be influenced by trade. On the other hand, since incomes of Third World farmers are derived from production and trade, and not from direct income support from governments, Third World farmers will be totally vulnerable to changes in global trade patterns and international prices of agricultural commodities.

According to the AOA, India does not need to reduce its subsidies because India's AMS is below 10 percent (based on 1986-88 period), therefore India does not have a total AMS reduction commitment under the agreement. In fact, India's AMS is negative. However, agricultural subsidies related to water and power are being removed under World Bank adjustment policies. Thus, the support to farmers is declining, whereas the support and subsidies to industries providing inputs for agriculture are increasing. For example, the subsidies for Urea increased from *Rs. 16.7* billion in 1996-97 to *Rs. 20* billion budgeted for 1997-98. Trade liberalization has, therefore, left India with an additional burden just for subsidies for chemical fertilizers. The politics of subsidies in the WTO is therefore clearly weighted in favor of industry and northern agribusiness and against farmers, especially those of the Third World.[16]

Market Access

The WTO agreement on the import of food is entitled "market access" and is covered by Part III, Articles 4 and 5 and Annexure 3. All signatory countries must convert quantitative restrictions and other non-tariff measures into ordinary customs duties. This is referred to as "tariffication." Countries have to provide minimum market access, beginning with 1 percent of the domestic consumption in the first year of the implementation period, to be increased in equal annual installments to 2 percent at the beginning of the fifth year. After that, it has to be increased to 4 percent. "Market access opportunities" are defined as "imports as a percentage of the corresponding domestic consumption."

Customs and other duties on imports are to be reduced by 36 percent (24 percent for developing countries) to facilitate imports at cheaper prices. Customs and other duties shall not exceed one-third of the level of the customs duties, i.e., these duties will be calculated on the basis of the difference between the import price and the trigger price. (The trigger price is the average of 1986 to 1988 prices.) Removal of quantitative restrictions on imports of agricultural commodities is a major goal of trade liberalization.

While the governments of Third World countries are busy meeting schedules, calculating AMS, and fighting disputes, the corporations are taking over their agricultural systems. Arithmetic has been made a mode of conquest and a source of distraction in the WTO. Government energy is focused on the arithmetic of dismantling, and corporate energy is focused on the politics of takeover.

According to the UN's Food and Agriculture Organization (FAO), as a result of trade liberalization measures, Africa's food import bill will go up from $8.4 billion to $14.9 billion by the year 2000. For Latin America and the Caribbean, the value of increased imports is $0.9 billion. For the Far East, the import bill will increase by $4.1 billion. For the Near East, the import bill will increase to $27 billion and the trade gap will widen from US$11 to US$19 billion by the year 2000.[17]

Export Competition
Articles 8-11 of the AOA deal with exports under the title "Export Competition." The official justification for the AOA is the removal of export subsidies that have facilitated the sale of large European Union and U.S. surpluses on the world market. The main elements of the export subsidy commitments are as follows:

◆   Export subsidies, measured in terms of both the volume of subsidized exports, and in terms of budgetary expenditure on subsidies, have been capped.

- Developed countries are committed to reducing the volume of subsidized exports by 21 percent and the expenditure on subsidies by 36 percent, both over a six-year period (1995-2000).

- For developing countries, the reduction commitments are 14 percent and 24 percent for volume and expenditure respectively, while the implementation period (1995-2004) lasts ten years rather than six. However, governments of developing countries can continue to subsidize the cost of marketing exports of agricultural products including handling, upgrading, and other processing costs and the costs of international transport and freight. The costs of internal transport and freight charges on export shipments can continue to receive subsidies.

- The agreement precludes export bans even in years of domestic shortages.

While the liberalization of exports was justified by the argument that Northern agricultural markets would open up to India, India's exports to Europe have actually declined from 13 percent to 6 percent. One of the reasons for this is because high subsidies and protectionist barriers are still largely maintained in the North. Thus, trade liberalization is a uni-directional phenomenon that opens markets in the South for Northern business and corporations but closes markets in the North for trade from the South.

Direct export subsidies of $14.5 billion will still be allowed under the AOA. The export subsidies that are allowed to developing countries are not subsidies to Third World farmers or the poor, because farmers do not export, companies do. They are subsidies that go to commercial and corporate interests, since it is northern agribusiness corporations which are expanding in the Third World, the exempted export subsidies for developing countries are again export subsidies to global corporations. Third World governments are, therefore, allowed to support global corporations but not their farmers and the poor since they can continue to subsidize transport, processing and marketing.

Transnational corporations therefore gain both from northern subsidies and southern subsidies under WTO rules. Further, northern subsidies to agribusiness have not been touched. Since the WTO was established, the United States has expanded export credit and marketing promotion programs. Even IMF loans to Third World countries have been used for export subsidies to U.S. agribusiness.

Dan Glickman, U.S. secretary of Agriculture, has stated, "The main reason we have not lost more exports to Asia is because the [U.S. Department of Agriculture] extended U.S. $2.1 billion in export credit guarantees. Without IMF actions another $2 billion in agricultural exports would have been at great risk in the short-term and far larger amounts in the long term." [18]

The 1996 U.S. Farm Bill mandated $5.5 billion for export promotion. An additional $1 billion was granted for promoting sales to "emerging markets." Another $90 million has been allocated for Market Access Programs which go to food and agriculture corporations for product promotion abroad.

WTO rules are for preserving and enhancing corporate subsidies and withdrawing support to farmers and rural communities whether they refer to Domestic Support, Market Access or Export Competition. Protection of farmers' livelihoods, food security, and sustainable agriculture requires major changes in the AOA.

Upcoming Review of the AOA
The United States has already announced that further liberalization of agriculture will be its top priority at the WTO Ministerial meeting in Seattle. However, the AOA does provide an opportunity to challenge this approach, which is a requirement (Article 20) that parties review the Agreement.

While Article 20 lays out the requirement for a review, the preamble of the Agreement provides an opening for challenging the current AOA on the basis of food security and environmental concerns. The preamble, in part, states:

Commitments under the reform program should be made in an equitable way among all Members, having regard to non-trade concerns, including food security and the need to protect the environment; having regard to the agreement that special and differential treatment for developing countries is an integral element of the negotiations, and taking into account the possible negative effects of the implementation of the reform program on least developed and net food-importing countries.

Recommendations regarding the AOA review:

1. The primary non-trade concerns identified in the AOA preamble are food security and sustainability. The impact of trade liberalization on both has been negative. On this basis, an exemption clause should be introduced in the WTO that allows countries to keep agriculture outside trade liberalization rules, allows them to support their agriculture and environment, and allows national sovereignty over policies for food security and sustainability.

2. The reviewed and amended AOA should have only two roles after agriculture has been exempted on food security grounds. Firstly, to remove export subsidies in all forms, including the disguised subsidies in export guarantee and credit schemes, investment, and transport. It is not the support at domestic levels that creates the problem of dumping. It is a combination of export subsidies and forced imports. If export subsidies were removed and countries were allowed to maintain quantitative restrictions for food security, not just for balance of payments purposes, domestic support would not translate into dumping and consequent destruction of local markets and local livelihoods.

3. The second important role of the AOA should be to prevent monopolies such as those enjoyed by Cargill in trade and those enjoyed by Monsanto in seeds. Consolidation and

integration at all levels has led to monopoly conditions both at the level of inputs and at the level of food processing and distribution systems. Anti-monopoly, anti-trust laws should be introduced in agriculture.

4. The review process should include the following steps:

◆ Freeze on all further trade liberalization of agriculture and on implementation of current rules.

◆ Two-year review of impact of trade liberalization on food security and sustainability.

◆ Exempt agriculture from trade liberalization on the grounds of food security and sustainability and introduce anti-monopoly clauses.

Need for a New Paradigm

For these proposals to be realized, we need to build a movement around a new paradigm for food and agriculture that identifies trade liberalization itself as the cause of environmental degradation and loss of livelihoods for the poor in the South. Even where exports are possible, they are often at heavy social and ecological cost to commodities from the South. Therefore, the rules of the WTO must change and imports and exports should not be forced and food and agriculture must be removed and exempted from the "discipline" of free trade so that it can serve the objectives of food security and environmental protection.

Trade cannot, and must not be made the highest objective to govern food systems because this implies rule of trading interests i.e., the rule of global corporations. Corporations view food as a source of profits, not a source life and livelihoods. Because their profits can grow only by destroying livelihoods and self-provisioning systems of seed production and food production, globalization of trade in agriculture implies genocide. Revising free trade logic is necessary if life of humans and other species is to be protected.

Protection of domestic agriculture needs to be recognized as a food security imperative, and WTO rules should not undermine food security by destroying local agriculture and food systems through subsidized dumping. Putting up tariff barriers to genocide is a moral imperative.

Third World countries are now locked into growing export crops because of debt and balance of payment crises. Their exports should be facilitated through fair trade arrangements, i.e., trade that is not based on environmental destruction and displacement of small peasants and destruction of local food economies. Fair trade will not be ensured by the free trade rules of market access of WTO which can be forced on the South but not on the North. It needs a spirit of solidarity and rules of cooperation. Genocidal market competition needs to be replaced by ethical trading, fair trade, and new rules of North-South cooperation. We need to build a movement to allow countries to exclude food and agriculture from free-trade arrangements, so that ecological and social justice concerns can be the basis of how food is produced, distributed, and consumed.

C. TRIPs AND BIOPIRACY

IN ADDITION TO THE AOA, the WTO threatens Third World food and agriculture through the Trade Related Intellectual Property Rights (TRIPs) agreement, which was introduced during the Uruguay Round of GATT. This agreement sets enforceable global rules on patents, copyrights, and trademarks. TRIPs rules extend to living resources, so that genes, cells, seeds, plants, and animals can now be patented and "owned" as intellectual property.[19] As a result, developing countries are being forced to reorganize their production and consumption patterns to allow monopolies by a handful of so-called "Life Sciences" corporations that are in reality peddlers of death.

History of Intellectual Property Rights

To understand the flaws of TRIPs, it is important to know that this agreement is essentially the globalization of western patent laws that historically have been used as instruments of conquest. The word "patents" derives from "letters patent"—the open letters granted by European sovereigns to conquer foreign lands or to obtain import monopolies. Christopher Columbus derived his right to the conquest of the Americas through the letter patent granted to him by Queen Isabel and King Ferdinand.[20]

In the United States, patent laws were originally a patchwork of state laws that did not offer protection for the patentee outside the state in which it had been granted. This changed in 1787, when members of the Constitutional Convention institutionalized a national statute. The politicians were convinced that a single federal patent law would serve the fledgling nation and its inventors far more effectively than the existing state patents. One outcome was that broad patents were granted in the United States for steamboats—in spite of the steam engine having been invented and patented by James Watt in Scotland fifteen years before.

The United States has continued to ignore the pre-existence and use of inventions in other countries when granting patents. Thus, paradoxically, a legal system aimed at preventing "intellectual piracy" is itself based on legitimizing piracy. This system is codified in Section 102 of the U.S. Patent Act of 1952, which denies patents for inventions that are in use in the United States but allows patents for inventions in use in other countries unless they have been described in a publication. If, for example, someone in Europe were operating a machine and you, in good faith, independently and without knowledge of its existence, developed your own invention that was essentially the same machine, that fact would not prevent you from obtaining a patent in the United States.

In addition, the United States has created unilateral instruments such as clause Special 301 in its Trade Act to force other countries to follow its patent laws. Thus, a country that depended on borrowed knowledge for its own development of industrial power has acted to block such transfer of knowledge and technology to other countries.

Introduction of TRIPs

During the Uruguay Round of the GATT, the United States introduced its flawed patent system into the WTO, and thus imposed it on the rest of the world. U.S. corporations have admitted that they drafted and lobbied on behalf of TRIPs. As a Monsanto spokesman said, "The industries and traders of world commerce have played simultaneously the role of patients, the diagnosticians, and prescribing physicians."

TRIPs not only made intellectual property rights (IPR) laws global geographically, but also removed ethical boundaries by including life forms and biodiversity into patentable subject matter. Living organisms and life forms that are self-creating were thus redefined as machines and artifacts made and invented by the patentee. Intellectual property rights and patents then give the patent holder a monopolistic right to prevent others from making, using, or selling seeds. Seed saving by farmers has now been redefined from a sacred duty to a criminal offence of stealing "property." Article 27.3 (b) of the TRIPs agreement, which relates to patents on living resources, was basically pushed by the "Life Science" companies to establish themselves as Lords of Life.

The chemical companies of the world have bought up seed and biotechnology companies and reorganized themselves as Life Science corporations, claiming patents on genes, seeds, plants and animals. Ciba Geigy and Sandoz have combined to form Novartis; Hoechst has joined with Rhone Poulenc to form Aventis; Zeneca has merged with Astia; Dupont has bought up Pioneer HiBred; and Monsantio now owns Cargill seeds, DeKalb, Calgene, Agracetus, Delta and Pine Land, Holden, and

Asgrow. Eighty percent of all genetically engineered seeds planted are Monsanto's "intellectual property." And Monsanto owns broad species patents on cotton, mustard, soyabean—crops that were not "invented" or "created" by Monsanto but have been evolved over centuries of innovation by farmers of India and East Asia working in close partnership with biodiversity gifted by nature.

There are three perversions inherent in patents on living material:

1. Ethical perversion

This refers to the claim that seeds, plants, sheep, cows, or human cell lines are nothing but "products of the mind" "created" by Monsanto, Novartis, Ian Wilmut or PPL. Living organisms have their intrinsic self-organization, they make themselves, and hence cannot be reduced to the status of "inventions" and "creations" of patent holders. They cannot be "owned" as private property because they are our ecological kin, not just "genetic mines."

2. Criminalization of Saving and Sharing Seeds

The recognition of corporations as "owners" of seed through intellectual property rights converts farmers into "thieves" when they save seed or share it with neighbors. Monsanto hires detectives to chase farmers who might be engaging in such "theft."

3. Encourages Biopiracy

"Biopiracy" is the theft of biodiversity and indigenous knowledge through patents. Biopiracy deprives the South in three ways:

◆ It creates a false claim to novelty and invention, even though the knowledge has evolved since ancient times. Thus, biopiracy is intellectual theft, which robs Third World people of their creativity and their intellectual resources.

◆ It diverts scarce biological resources to monopoly control of corporations, depriving local communities and indigenous practitioners. Thus, biopiracy is resource theft from the poorest two thirds of humanity who depend on biodiversity for their livelihoods and basic needs.

◆ It creates market monopolies and excludes the original inno-vators from their rightful share of local, national, and international markets. Instead of preventing this organized economic theft, WTO rules protect the powerful and punish the victims. In a dispute initiated by the United States against India, the WTO forced India to change its patent laws and grant exclusive marketing rights to foreign corpo-rations on the basis of foreign patents. Since many of these patents are based on biopiracy, the WTO is in fact promot-ing piracy through patents.

Over time, the consequences of TRIPs for the South's biodi-versity and southern people's rights to their diversity will be severe. No one will be able to produce or reproduce patented agricultural, medicinal, or animal products freely, thus eroding livelihoods of small producers and preventing the poor from using their own resources and knowledge to meet their basic needs of health and nutrition. Royalties for their use will have to be paid to the patentees and unauthorized production will be penalized, thus increasing the debt burden.

Indian farmers, traditional practitioners, and traders will lose their market share in local, national and global markets. For example, recently the U.S. government granted a patent for the anti-diabetic properties of karela, jamun, and brinjal to two non-resident Indians, Onkar S. Tomer and Kripanath Borah, and their colleague Peter Gloniski. The use of these substances for control of diabetes is everyday knowledge and practice in India. Their medical use is documented in authoritative treatises like the "Wealth of India," the "Compendium of Indian Medicinal Plants" and the "Treatise on Indian Medicinal Plants."

If there were only one or two cases of such false claims to invention on the basis of biopiracy, they could be called an error.

However, biopiracy is an epidemic. Neem, haldi, pepper, harar, bahera, amla, mustard, basmati, ginger, castor, jaramla, amaltas and new karela and jamun have all been patented. The problem is not, as was made out to be in the case of turmeric, an error made by a patent clerk. The problem is deep and systemic. And it calls for a systemic change, not case-by-case challenges.

Some have suggested that biopiracy happens because Indian knowledge is not documented. That is far from true. Indigenous knowledge in India has been systematically documented, and this in fact has made piracy easier. And even the folk knowledge orally held by local communities deserves to be recognized as collective, cumulative innovation. The ignorance of such knowledge in the United States should not be allowed to treat piracy as invention.

The potential costs of biopiracy to the Third World poor are very high since two thirds of the people in the South depend on free access to biodiversity for their livelihoods and needs. Seventy percent of seed in India is saved or shared farmers' seed; 70 percent of healing is based on indigenous medicine using local plants.

If a patent system that is supposed to reward inventiveness and creativity systematically rewards piracy, if a patent system fails to honestly apply criteria of novelty and nonobviousness in the granting of patents related to indigenous knowledge, then the system is flawed, and it needs to change. It cannot be the basis of granting patents or establishing exclusive marketing rights. The problem of biopiracy is a result of Western-style IPR systems, not the absence of such IPR systems in India. Therefore, the implementation of TRIPs, which is based on the U.S.-style patent regimes, should be immediately stopped and its review started.

The survival of the anachronistic Art. 102 of the U.S. Patent Law thus enables the United States to pirate knowledge freely from other countries, patent it, and then fiercely protect this stolen knowledge as "intellectual property." Knowledge flows freely into the United States but is prevented from flowing freely out of the United States. If biopiracy is to stop, then the U.S. patent laws must change, and Article 102 must be redrafted to recognize *prior art* of other countries. This is especially important given that U.S. patent laws have been globalized through the TRIPs agreement of the WTO.

Upcoming Review of TRIPs

In 1999, Article 27.3 (b) of the TRIPs agreement is scheduled to come up for review. This is the article that most directly impacts indigenous knowledge because it relates to living resources and biodiversity. In the year 2000, countries can also call for an amendment of TRIPs as a whole.

The review and amendment of TRIPs should begin with an examination of the deficiencies and weakness of western-style IPS systems. Instead of being pressured, as India has been, to implement a perverse IPR system through TRIPs, developing countries should lead a campaign in the WTO for review and amendment of the system. In the meantime, these countries should freeze the implementation of TRIPs. While TRIPs implementation is frozen, they should make domestic laws that protect indigenous knowledge as the common property of the people, and as a national heritage.

The implementation of the Convention on Biological Diversity (CBD) enables us to do this. Because CBD is also an international treaty, protecting indigenous knowledge via a Biodiversity Act does not violate international obligations. In fact, removing the inconsistencies between TRIPs and CBD should be an important part of the international campaign for the review and amendment of TRIPs.

Piracy of indigenous knowledge will continue until patent laws directly address this issue, exclude patents on indigenous knowledge and trivial modifications of it, and create sui generis systems for the protection of collective, cumulative innovation.

The protection of diverse knowledge systems requires a diversity of IPR systems, including systems that do not reduce knowledge and innovation to private property for monopolistic profits. Systems of common property in knowledge need to be evolved for preserving the integrity of indigenous knowledge systems on the basis of which our everyday survival is based.

Neither TRIPs nor the U.S. patent law recognize knowledge as a "commons," nor do they recognize the collective, cumulative innovation embodied in indigenous knowledge systems. Thus, if indigenous knowledge is to be protected, then TRIPs and U.S. patent laws must change. Nothing less than an overhaul of western-style IPR systems with their intrinsic weaknesses will stop the epidemic of biopiracy. And if biopiracy is not stopped, the every day survival of ordinary Indians will be threatened, as over time our indigenous knowledge and resources will be used to make patented commodities for global trade. Global corporate profits will grow at the cost of the food rights, health rights, and knowledge rights of one billion Indians, two thirds of whom are too poor to meet their needs through the global market place.

Patents on indigenous knowledge and uses of plants is an "enclosure" of the intellectual and biological commons on which the poor depend. Robbed of their rights and entitlements to freely use nature's capital because that is the only capital they have access to, the poor in the Third World will be pushed to extinction. Like the diverse species on which they depend, they too are a threatened species.

Citizens' Movements

"No patents on life" movements and movements against bio-piracy are already strong in the North and South. These citizens initiatives need to be the basis of the TRIPs to exclude life from patents and IPR monopolies. In India, Navdanya (the movement for conservation of native seeds) has catalyzed broad-based alliances for food freedom and seed freedom with farmers' groups, women's groups, and environmental groups. The Bija Satyagraha or Seed Satyagraha is the non-cooperation movement against patents on life, genetic engineering of crops and corporate monopolies in agriculture. The "Jaiv Panchayat" movement or the Living Democracy movement focuses on the protection of all species and for local democratic control on biodiversity and indigenous knowledge.

During Freedom Week, August 9-15, 1999, the Living Democracy movement from more than 500 village communities sent notices to biopirates such as W.R. Grace, which has claimed the use of neem as pesticide as its invention; Monsanto, whose subsidiary Calgene has patents on mustard and castor; and RiceTec, which has a patent on basmati. Notices have also been sent to the WTO for overstepping its jurisdiction because under traditional legal systems and under the Indian Constitution, the local community (*gram sabha*) is the highest competent authority on matters related to biodiversity.

Another peoples' organization, *Hamara Roti, Hamara Azadi* (Our Bread, Our Freedom), brings together environmentalists, women, farmers, workers, and students. The coalition is increasing awareness of corporations such as Monsanto and Cargill, which are trying to control Indian agriculture and are destroying millions of livelihoods in food production and food processing, destroying the rich biological and cultural diversity of our agricultural and food systems, and destroying the ecologically sustainable consumption patterns. On August 13, 1999, protestors at the Delhi offices of Monsanto and Cargill demanded that the corporations divest from India and stop their ecocide and genocide.

The TRIPs agreement has an impact on biodiversity and thus subverts our democratic rights to our biodiversity and indigenous knowledge. Biodiversity should stay in the hands of local communities. This is a right recognized in our traditions and enshrined in our Constitution. The WTO is destroying our democratic decision-making structures by forcing the government to undo the Panchayati rights of the people in decentralized democratic structures through the implementation of TRIPs. Our campaign for the review of TRIPs will be to designate the *gram sabha*, or local community, as the competent authority for the defense of biodiversity and the protection of indigenous knowledge as collective and cumulative innovation.

CONCLUSION

THE REAL MILLENNIUM ROUND for the WTO is the beginning of a new democratic debate about the future of the earth and the future of its people. The centralized, undemocratic rules and structures of the WTO that are establishing global corporate rule based on monopolies and monocultures need to give way to an earth democracy supported by decentralization and diversity. The rights of all species and the rights of all peoples must come before the rights of corporations to make limitless profits through limitless destruction.

Free trade is not leading to freedom. It is leading to slavery. Diverse life forms are being enslaved through patents on life, farmers are being enslaved into high-tech slavery, and countries are being enslaved into debt and dependence and destruction of their domestic economies.

We want a new millennium based on economic democracy, not economic totalitarianism. The future is possible for humans and other species only if the principles of competition, organized greed, commodification of all life, monocultures and monopolies, and centralized global corporate control of our daily lives enshrined in the WTO are replaced by the principles of protection of people and nature, the obligation of giving and sharing diversity, and the decentralization and self-organization enshrined in our diverse cultures and national constitutions.

The WTO rules violate principles of human rights and ecological survival. They violate rules of justice and sustainability. They are rules of warfare against the people and the planet. Changing these rules is the most important democratic and human rights struggle of our times. It is a matter of survival.

FOOTNOTES

1. Vandana Shiva, "Globalization of Agriculture and the Growth of Food Insecurity," Report of International Conference on Globalization, Food Security and Sustainable Agriculture, RFSTE, 1996.

2. Vandana Shiva and Afsar H. Jafri, "Seeds of Suicide: The Ecological and Human Costs of Globalization of Agriculture," RFSTE, 1998.

3. Vandana Shiva, Afsar H. Jafri & Ashok Emani, : "Globalization and The Threat to Seed Security: The Case of Transgenic Cotton Trials in India," EPW, March 1999).

4. Ibid.

5. Supreme Course Case, RFSTE, Writ Petition No.71,1999.

6. Vandana Shiva, "Betting on Biodiversity: Why Genetic Engineering Will Not Feed the Hungry," RFSTE, 1998.

7. Vandana Shiva and Gurpreet Karir, "Towards Sustainable Aquaculture: Chenmmeenkettu," RFSTE, 1997.

8. Vandana Shiva , Afsar H. Jafri and Gitanjali Bedi, "The Ecoomic Cost of Economic Globalization: The Indian Experience," RFSTE, 1997.

9. Maneka Gandhi, "The Crimes of Al-kabir," People for Animals Newsletter, May 1995).

10. Vandana Shiva (Ed), "Globalization and Agriculture," SAGE Publications (forthcoming).

11. "Urban poor find food hard to come by," Times of India, 9 July 1999.

12. Vandana Shiva, "Mustard or Soy? The Future of India's Edible Oil Culture," Navdanya, 1998

13. Ibid.

14. CII & McKinsey, FAIDA, 1998.

15. "Monsanto: Peddling "Life Sciences" or "Death Sciences?" RFSTE, 1998.

16. WTO Trade Policy Review India, WT/TPR/S/33WTO.

17. Contract Agreement of Bioseed Research India Private Limited.

18. "Inside U.S. Trade," Release No. 008998, Remarks of Secretary, Dan Glickman, 1998, Agricultural Outlook, Washington D.C., February 23, 1998.

19. Vandana Shiva, Biopiracy: The Plunder of Nature and Knowledge, South End Press, USA 1997 and RFSTE, New Delhi, 1998.

20. Ibid.

IMPLICATIONS FOR DEVELOPING AND LEAST DEVELOPED COUNTRIES

Dot Keet

This is an abbreviated version of a paper presented by Dot Keet at a November 1998 conference on "The WTO: Law and Development in South Africa" at the University of the Western Cape, South Africa. Keet is a senior researcher at this university's Centre for Southern African Studies and a researcher/analyst and activist in the Alternative Information and Development Center (aidc@iafrica.com) in Cape Town.

Keet's analysis of the World Trade Organization is rooted in the experiences of the countries of Africa—the region of the world that is most marginalized in the global economy. She describes how the developed nations have taken advantage of the weaknesses of Africa's developing countries to manipulate and abuse the multilateral rules-based system. According to Keet, the world's poorest nations are handicapped in trade negotiations not only by their lack of experience and resources, but even more fundamentally because they have little to offer in the complex deal making over reciprocal tariff reductions and other mutual concessions. She also points out the potential threats that the WTO poses to the right of African nations to determine their own development strategies. For example, in her country of South Africa, laws to support disadvantaged sections of the population through preferential government contracting could be undermined by proposed WTO investment rules.

DASHED EXPECTATIONS
IN DEVELOPING COUNTRIES

IT WAS NOT UNTIL the later phases of the prolonged Uruguay Round that the strategic purposes of the central World Trade Organization (WTO) agreements gradually became evident to the developing countries that participated in the negotiations. In this they were assisted by the revelations and analyses of close observers [Ragnavan, 1990] and direct participants in the process [Shahin, 1996; Das, 1998] on their behalf.[1] In fact, for much of the Uruguay Round, most of the developing country representatives were little more than spectators at the so-called multilateral —but in practice often bilateral—bargaining and the agreements being constructed by the most powerful developed countries.[2]

The weak participation and impact of the developing countries in the Uruguay Round was partially owing to their fewer numbers,[3] but was more owing to their limited experience in multilateral negotiations—although with some exceptions, such as India. This lack of impact was also attributable to their failure to foresee the new strategic thrust of the highly industrialized countries, and the new purposes to which their governments were aiming to turn the old General Agreement on Tariffs and Trade (GATT) into the new WTO. However, the developing countries also erred in approaching the Uruguay Round negotiations with very limited objectives and in making very narrowly focused interventions in the discussions, if any at all.

With hindsight, the developing countries appeared overly reliant upon and too trustful in their expectations of the new round of negotiations. The developing countries that had clearly identified aims perceived the multilateral, multisectoral liberalization negotiations of the Uruguay Round as an important opportunity to promote their specific interests and obtain positive responses to their long-standing grievances in the existing international trade regime. Their first aim was to end the exclusions and secure full access for their few globally competitive manufactured exports—mainly textiles and clothing—into the high consumer markets of the rich developed countries. The second major concern was that their other important exports—from the agricultural sector—should be incorporated into GATT, which had hitherto only covered manufactured goods of interest to the more industrialized countries. The developing countries achieved neither of these aims, except as longer term prospects into the new millennium.

The third motivation of many developing countries in going along with the largely unsatisfactory Uruguay Round negotiations, and in welcoming the establishment of the WTO at the end, was their optimistic expectation that the new "multilateral rules-based system" for international trade and other economic relations would be set in motion through the WTO. It was anticipated that this would, *inter alia*, bring to an end the unilateral measures and pressures, largely by the strongest governments against weaker—although also between the developed countries themselves—that had long characterized international economic relations. Within the new multilateral framework of rules and regulations, all members would be able—and would be expected—to settle their trade and trade-related disagreements through the Dispute Resolution Undertaking (DSU) that emerged from the Uruguay Round.

ABUSES OF THE MULTILATERAL RULES-BASED SYSTEM BY DEVELOPED COUNTRIES

THE EXPERIENCE OF THE WEAKER countries with the DSU over the five years since the creation of the WTO has not been as positive as was expected. The complexity of the issues and the procedures, and the capacity of stronger countries/companies to prolong the dispute panel's processes,[4] means that weaker complainants can be irreparably damaged in the interim, even if the WTO panel eventually rules in their favor. Weaker countries are also manifestly reluctant to pursue official DSU processes through the WTO—at one level owing to their lack of legal expertise and to the vast costs entailed in hiring international legal experts and researchers. At an underlying level, this caution is probably also due to their apprehension (arising from wider experience) about possible indirect reprisals by their stronger adversaries in other spheres and ways, should formal proceedings be instituted against them.

These, of course, have long been the dilemmas facing weaker parties in legal processes within national judicial systems all over the world. But the range of precautionary procedures, compensatory provisions, and corrective measures, such as legal aid, that have evolved in many national judicial systems to respond to such difficulties and inequities have not yet been incorporated into the WTO adjudication processes. Some of the procedural problems are gradually being addressed within the WTO—such as the professionalization of the panels, and the determination of time frames within which disputes must be resolved [EU, 1998]. There is also a proposal for a dedicated law centre, financed by the richer countries, to advise and assist weaker developing countries in the WTO.[5]

However, the bias against the weaker countries in the new WTO DSU is evident more fundamentally in the very different implications of the theoretical right of aggrieved parties to impose WTO-approved sanctions on transgressors. The formalistic nature of the "equal rights and treatment" of all members within the WTO is manifest in the limited utility, or indeed the very feasibility, of such authorized counter-actions being imposed by weak governments against the strong. The impact of such putative measures upon the strongest economies would invariably be limited, but the economic and political risks would be considerable to the weaker implementers of such sanctions. This disability is reinforced by the fact that DSU processes in the WTO are designed to deal with disputes between the contracting parties as purely bilateral matters. Apart from hypothetical collective "moral pressures"—for what they are worth in the ruthless sphere of international trade relations—the system does not have a multilateral mechanism of effective enforcement [Das, 1998b]. The observance and efficacy of panel findings is largely related to economic power and political influence or, in rare instances, calculated decisions about the advantages of upholding the wider multilateral rules-based system. This was manifest even in the conduct of the European Union (EU) in its recent "banana dispute" with the United States in the WTO.

The more general threat to the so-called multilateral rules-based system is that some powerful governments—mainly, but not only the United States—continue to act unilaterally when it is considered necessary to protect or promote national economic and even political interests. Washington routinely applies its own 301 trade legislation to threaten other countries, and even resorts to extraterritorial enforcement of particular national economic laws to serve strategic U.S. objectives.[6] The U.S. government is also noted for its frequent recourse to damaging antidumping actions and countervailing measures against foreign imports when required to do so by domestic industries to protect them against allegedly unfair competitors. This may be within the letter of the relevant WTO agreements, but goes against the spirit of the open, free-trade, competitive global economy purportedly being promoted by the new world trade regime. On the other hand, it is extremely difficult for weaker countries lacking the necessary financial, legal, trade monitoring, and industrial research facilities to institute their own antidumping actions against powerful economies such as the United States and the EU, even when they might possibly have a strong case.[7]

The United States is not the only country to flout the letter and spirit of the new "global multilateralism." Industrialized countries in the Organization for Economic Cooperation and Development (OECD) attempted, through their own less-than-global multilateral negotiations, to create a new Multilateral Agreement on Investment (MAI) outside of the WTO, for the full and unfettered operation of foreign investors and transnational corporations (TNCs) throughout the world [EC, 1995]. This strategy was effectively exposed and energetically opposed by a global alliance of civil society organizations that succeeded in dividing the OECD governments, such that the French government officially withdrew its support and the process was suspended. Had this not happened, the MAI would have been presented, in form multilaterally, but in essence unilaterally, to all the other countries seeking foreign investment [Abugre, 1997]. The EU, Japan, and other governments, under continuing pressure from their global financial corporations and TNCs, are now aiming to get their (renamed) Multilateral Investment Agreement (MIA) integrated into and approved within the "more fully multilateral" and "bottom-up" processes of the WTO. However this, in turn, raises further critical questions with respect to the functioning of the WTO, per se.[8]

In addition to the evasions illustrated above, the "multilateral" nature of decisionmaking in the WTO itself has been most pervasively contradicted by the highly nontransparent, noninclusive processes within the organization, and the backroom deals between the most powerful countries, which are then presented to the rest of the WTO membership as a *de facto* consensus to be endorsed [Khor, 1999]. Tactical alliances between smaller groups of like-minded countries, or those with specific interests in common, may be an intrinsic part of multilateral negotiations.

But, in the case of the WTO, the influence of specific groups of the more influential countries is reinforced by the marked susceptibility—and even the unofficial "accountability"—of the WTO director general and the secretariat to the most powerful member states.[9] However, quite apart from this manifestation of global power politics, the more fundamental, structural bias of the WTO resides in the WTO secretariat's "impartial" application of the tendentious agreements already secured by those states and the official endorsement and promotion by the WTO of the assumptions of the global neoliberal paradigm [WTO,1996].

The WTO secretariat's accommodation to the most powerful states is also evident in the prolonged failure of the organization in the first five years of its existence to energetically pursue and secure the effective implementation of the formal undertakings made, and the assurances given, to the lesser and least developed countries by the industrialized country governments in the Final Act of the Uruguay Round in Marrakesh. The "Marrakesh Ministerial Decision on Measures in Favor of Least Developed Countries," and "Measures Concerning the Possible Negative Effect of the Agricultural Reform Programme on Net Food Importing Countries" were the belated acknowledgement, by the main beneficiaries of the Uruguay Round, of the marginalization of the weaker countries and the predicted (or what they defined as the "possible") prejudicial effects of the new global trade regime upon them.

MARGINALIZATION FOR LEAST DEVELOPED COUNTRIES

MOST OF THE LESSER DEVELOPED countries, and the majority of theUnited Nation's (UN) officially designated forty-eight Least Developed Countries (LDCs) worldwide, are in Africa. These countries, together designated as Lesser and Least Developed

Countries (LLDCs) in this paper,[10] had an extremely weak presence throughout the Uruguay Round. Their interests and particular needs were virtually ignored until the penultimate phases, when UNCTAD and other UN agencies stepped in to assist them. The preliminary assessment of UN agencies—subsequently endorsed in general terms by World Bank and OECD studies—was that, although the Uruguay Round would indeed encourage a massive expansion in global trade, this would be very unevenly distributed according to the production and trade capacities of the respective countries. Weaker countries, above all in Africa, would actually lose out from global trade liberalization, in absolute as well as relative terms. According to such studies, the immediate effects of the increasingly liberalized global trade regime would be overwhelmingly to the advantage of the most highly developed countries. The estimates include a combined $139 billion trade expansion for the EU, the United States, and Japan. But weaker economies would suffer absolute losses, such as $2.6 billion in sub-Saharan Africa, $1.6 billion in North Africa and the Mediterranean, and $1.9 billion in Indonesia [OXFAM, 1998].

Even before the predictions of their weakening performance in the global free trade system, the weak participation by the LLDCs in the Uruguay Round was evident. (It is interesting to note that in the whole of sub-Saharan Africa, only colonial Southern Rhodesia and the Union of South Africa were members of GATT from its outset in 1948.) A fundamental problem was that they had little to "offer" in the complex, cross-cutting negotiations on reciprocal tariff reductions and other mutual concessions being agreed upon between the most highly developed countries. Some of the stronger developing countries in Asia and Latin America did make their own tariff reduction offers. South Africa (SA) also actually chose to make a tariff reduction offer in 1993 during the Uruguay Round commensurate with the status and obligations of a Developed Country a decision and designation still causing controversy within this country, and posing possible future constraints on the domestic policy options of the South African government. However, the LLDCs had little to "bargain with" in the multilateral Uruguay Round, largely because many of them had already unilaterally introduced extensive external trade liberalization under IMF/ World Bank structural adjustment programs. Furthermore, their extremely limited bargaining base simply reflected the low interest of the "majors" in what their economies had to offer at that stage.

Conversely, most LLDCs at that stage (and today) had little immediate capacity, or much to gain as actors from the major new agreements in the Uruguay Round for the liberalization of investment, trade in services, and so on. The few notable exceptions among developing countries are India, Malaysia, and other Southeast Asian countries, and, to some degree, South Africa.

The intrinsically weaker bargaining power of weaker economies in international trade negotiations —in terms of what they could reciprocate in order to benefit from the trade liberalization of other economies—had long been acknowledged within GATT. Thus, key articles in Part IV on Trade and Development (endorsed in 1966) enshrined a "nonreciprocity clause" for developing and especially least developed countries. This meant that they could benefit from better trade access even if they did not have much to offer in return. What is more, this clause applies not only to trade but to other safeguard actions taken by such countries for development purposes. Exemption from the reciprocity obligation was not sufficient, however, to compensate for the systemic imbalances in the processes and products of international trade negotiations. Nor were such temporary concessions a sufficient response to the very uneven levels of development between the participating economies. Thus, the 1979 Tokyo Round of GATT incorporated a highly significant "enabling clause" on "Differential and More Favorable Treatment, Reciprocity and Fuller Participation of Developing Countries."

These and other counterbalancing, or compensatory, provisions within GATT toward developing countries were carried over into the WTO. They have come to be known as "special and differential terms" (SDTs) and include greater flexibility with regard to certain WTO obligations, such as the use of subsidies; more favorable thresholds, as with antidumping actions; and longer time frames for the implementation of WTO undertakings, such as with TRIPs, with the right to further extensions if duly motivated. The three broad objectives of these terms are to provide these economies with:

◆ Enhanced Market Access and Trade Promotion—not only through the generalized system of preferences (GSP), but through preferential duty-free terms for the LDCs, if this is duly motivated; in addition to their right to enjoy intraregional preferences, if they are part of regional trade agreements;

◆ Discretion in the Domestic Use of Certain Policy Instruments —including the employment of tariffs as safeguards when necessary for balance of payments purposes or as interim protections for infant industries; or the use of government supports for the advancement of domestic production/capacities; and

◆ Support From the Developed Countries—not only in the form of technical and financial assistance, but in what is called "the best endeavour clause" to ensure that developing country interests are safeguarded when developed countries take certain measures in their own interests [UNCTAD, 1998].

However, in practice, the needs and special rights of developing countries often are simply ignored or sidelined by the onward thrust of the "majors" in WTO processes. And such established rights are also under increasing pressures both within and outside of the WTO. An illustration of the latter is that the

SDTs for developing countries, though enshrined in the WTO, are generally ignored and often directly contradicted in IMF and World Bank policy prescriptions. For example IMF/World Bank policies often prohibit governments under their sway from utilizing certain trade policy instruments, or require them to remove subsidies on food or small-scale agricultural production on the grounds of narrowly conceived and rigidly applied fiscal constraints.

Other external pressures, for example on the nonreciprocity rights of LLDCs, arise from the growing insistence of the EU that countries seeking better trade access to the EU market must enter into reciprocal free-trade agreements with the EU. Such reciprocal agreements are even a central component in the EU's proposed scenarios for its future relations with the African, Caribbean, and Pacific (ACP) members of the Lomé Convention. Similarly, the inclusion by the Euopean Community in its post-Lomé proposals of various trade-related measures—still under discussion and contention within the WTO—pose possible threats to the current rights and future exemptions in these spheres for these countries in the WTO [Keet, 1999].

Within the WTO itself there are also growing pressures to limit the coverage, scope, and duration of SDTs. "More advanced" developing countries, such as Peru, Argentina, and Brazil are being urged to disinvoke certain special rights and safeguards that they can presently use. Other developing countries applying to join the WTO since the Uruguay Round are being pressured to join on "commercially viable bases" rather than on established special and differential terms. There is also an insidious tendency within the WTO to refer to SDTs as if they apply only to LDCs in the narrowest definition of the term, which might have the main aim of excluding some of the more advanced developing countries but which would also exclude many lesser developing countries in Africa that still need to be able to use these rights.

Above all, the U.S. government is particularly insistent that a definitive time limit, namely the year 2005, be set on all current derogations from WTO obligations for LLDCs.[11]

FUTURE IMPLICATIONS FOR
DEVELOPING COUNTRIES

SOME OF THE IMMEDIATE PROBLEMS of developing countries in the WTO are apparently merely procedural, but at some are also technical, legal, economic, and political. The WTO incorporates not only dozens of specific agreements but thousands of pages of rules, regulations, and trade and tariff undertakings, going back fifty years to the beginning of GATT. The immediate difficulty facing new member countrie, with limited technical and legal capacities is the formal implementation of their obligations as contracting parties. This entails, for example, bringing various sections of their national legislation, such as their intellectual property regimes, into conformity with WTO requirements together with a host of other legal and institutional measures.

Many developing countries and especially LDCs have not been able to carry out such implementation and duly notify the WTO of their compliances and submissions. Until formal notifications are made, such countries are not in a position to access and implement their rights under specific agreements. In many cases, failure to effectively scrutinize and act on WTO agreements and regulations means that governments are not even fully aware of the rights that they have, and could utilize, in their domestic economies without fear of challenges or reprisals within the WTO. Rights in the WTO reside in their identification, affirmation and active application. If these rights are not utilized, such omissions are regarded as the conscious option of such governments. The concern of other contracting parties is not the unused rights of others but with unfullfilled obligations, and this is what they act on.

In addition to these implementation and realization challenges, the even more serious prejudice against the developing countries in the new trade regime under the WTO is that the focus of the negotiations was almost exclusively on products, services, and other issues of prime interest to the more developed countries. Not only did the specific products of export interest to developing countries largely remain outside of the trade liberalization but, because of their weak bargaining position, their particular exports actually continue to face widely prevalent tariff peaks and tariff escalations, which are higher than the tariffs obtaining on products mainly traded by and between the more developed countries; they have repeatedly demanded remedial action.[12]

Further outstanding disadvantages and future dangers for developing countries derive, somewhat paradoxically, from the pending liberalization of agricultural production and trade. On the one hand, this could end the subsidization and unfair trade competition from the EU and other agricultural exporters into developing countries. (Until this happens, such exports are placing insupportable competitive pressures on agricultural producers, including small-scale food producers, in developing economies.) On the other hand, with many Third World producers simultaneously being encouraged by the World Bank to switch from food production to commercial export crops—and with the periodic impact of droughts and other natural and man-made disasters—there is a growing tendency for many such countries to depend upon food imports, and even food aid, from the most highly industrialized countries. With the proposed liberalization of agricultural markets and the removal of agricultural production subsidies, there is a distinct possibility that such dependent, or "net food importing," countries could be seriously affected by rising global food prices and diminishing food aid from the decreasing agricultural production in some of the most developed countries, especially in Europe. This carries serious financial as well as broader economic, social, and political implications for many developing countries.

Among their many grievances and proposals, issues relating to the multifunctional role and requirements of their own agricultural production, food security, and more fair international trade remain a major preoccupation and demand of the developing countries within the WTO. However, even as they try to get responses on these and many other concerns from those that dominate the WTO, they are faced with constant new demands and further pressures from the same developed countries—most recently toward a full new multi sectoral Millennium Round.

NEW PRESSURES
FROM DEVELOPED COUNTRIES

IN THE AFTERMATH of the Uruguay Round not only have the developed countries barely responded to the problems and proposals of the developing countries, but the most powerful among them—most notably the United States—have continued to vigorously pursue their own interests and push their own priorities onto the WTO agenda. Thus, even as the developing countries came to the WTO 1996 Singapore Ministerial Conference (SMC) prepared to argue their case for the full implementation of outstanding commitments and agreements by the developed countries, and for a review of the impact of the recent Uruguay Round agreements, a new proposal from the United States for negotiations on information technology suddenly appeared on the SMC agenda, without any prior discussion in the preparatory meetings. The most developed countries and a few other "pivotal states," (including Singapore, as the host and a country with considerable information technology interests) withdrew into backroom negotiations. This left the remaining countries to address themselves in a mostly empty plenary hall. It was only toward the end of the conference that the exclusive negotiation group re-emerged with a "consensus" for a new Information Technology Agreement (ITA), which others were invited to accede to in due course, should they so decide.

A similar attempt was made by the United States to slip an entirely new agreement on electronic commerce into the second WTO Ministerial meeting in Geneva in May 1998 even though it was billed as a celebratory rather than a negotiating meeting. On that occasion, however, developing country delegates were more alert and managed to temporarily hold off a definitive Agreement on Electronic Commerce, subject to further analysis and discussion on the implications for their economies. It is on the basis of such experiences, in the context of the broader domination and biased utilization of WTO processes by the most powerful countries, that some developing country governments (and many non-governmental organizations from the developing and even developed countries) are now closely monitoring attempts to introduce ever more "new issues" into the WTO.

The U.S. government, Canada, the EU, and other European countries, such as Norway, have repeatedly mooted the possibility of introducing into the WTO "trade-related" agreements on labor and social rights, on environmental protection, and even on human rights, "good governance," and corruption, among other things. In the first instance, there are important questions to be faced as to whether multilateral trade negotiations and a global trade organization are appropriate instruments to deal with what are very complex, multidimensional problems. The links to trade are not clear or uncontested and the efficacy or desirability of applying trade sanctions to deal with such complex problems is questionable, particularly in light of the control of the WTO by the dominant powers.

The second question relates to the (overt and covert) motivations of developed countries on these issues. Some of the proposals by these government may have good intentions; however, for some governments, these proposals may simply be public relations postures to appease organized labor and other groups at home. Alternatively—or simultaneously—proposing to place such issues on the table may be a diversionary ploy while the real intention and more fundamental interest of such governments is to get other subjects of prime importance to their corporations and financial institutions, onto the formal WTO negotiating agenda. This is what seems to have happened at the SMC where the EU and the United States were apparently willing to "compromise" on the continued location of the proposed labor clause in the International Labor Organization.[13] However, as an undeclared but indirect counterbalance, the EU was particularly active in promoting an investment agreement to be taken up in the WTO and, together with the United States, in proposing other significant new "trade-related" issues for negotiation. These included competition policy and government procurement, the latter being a vast new area for lucrative business ventures for global corporations, larger even than merchandise trade.

The developing countries received these proposals with marked caution, undoubtedly based on their experiences with so-called multilateral negotiations in the WTO hitherto. However, their reservations were also based on the subjects themselves, because investment, competition policy, and government procurement play crucial roles in national economic and social development strategies [Khor, 1997]. In the case of South Africa, for example, having to open up all government contracts (national, provincial, local, and municipal) to international competition could prevent the government from fulfilling its aims to promote women; small, medium, and micro enterprises; and other disadvantaged sections of the population in the award of government contracts. This could affect diverse areas of national enterprise development, ranging from housing, school, and road and dam construction, to urban renewal projects and water and sanitation services, to hospital supplies and subcontracted services such as laundering, and even extending the provision to include of school meals and education.

The developing countries at the SMC would only agree that these new issues be made the subject of Working Group examinations. These, they insisted, would have to include research and analysis on the real "trade" connection, and the development implications of such subjects, and were to be undertaken in conjunction with appropriate specialized agencies such as UNCTAD. The further clear condition, incorporated into the final declaration that emerged from the SMC, was that such Working Groups would not be, and should not, automatically develop into negotiating groups on these issues. There are, however, strong indications that this is precisely what the EU, in particular, intended and intends. The Working Groups are gradually and insidiously being turned into *de facto* negotiating forums toward the inclusion of these contested issues into the proposed multisectoral Millenniuml Round; of which the EU is also one of the strongest proponents.

Whether these issues enter the WTO, and indeed whether there is to be a full new multisectoral round of negotiations, is currently being debated and informally negotiated between the permanent delegations (or those countries that can maintain permanent delegations) in Geneva, and will be formally decided or confirmed at the third Ministerial meeting in Seattle in December 1999. The possibilities or probabilities pose developing countries with diverse and extremely difficult political and legal challenges.

MILLENNIAL CHALLENGES

IN ADDITION TO the specific content and implications of the proposed "new issues" for negotiation, the following are some of the key principles; the specific procedural, technical, or tactical demand; and the broad legal, political, or strategic challenges facing developing countries, including South Africa.

A. SPECIAL AND DIFFERENTIAL TERMS

THE FIRST IMPERATIVE is the defense of the principles underpinning SDTs and the flexibility in terms of policy instruments and time-frames for developing countries that these terms provide. All countries that have such needs have to identify, apply, and, where necessary, argue for the extension of the coverage of these terms. They need also, collectively, to reject the external, *a priori* imposition of arbitrary limits and timeframes that do not arise out of and reflect the real economic processes, and broader social, environmental, political, and related dynamics within their national economies and emerging regions (such as SADC) [Keet,1998].

There are strong indications that developing countries are beginning to analyze and prioritize the defense of SDTs in their strategies vis-a-vis the WTO [Egypt,1998; OAU, 1998; India, 1998]. However, there is also a more proactive strategic potential in SDTs. The implicit recognition and even explicit acknowledgement (GATT, 1979) that it is inequitable to apply equal treatment to economies that are unequal has to be extended from merely providing a set of temporary technical/ legal provisions to compensating for the "imbalances" in the negotiations. The imbalances are much broader and more fundamental.

The neoliberal assumption that WTO rules for an open global economy will create a "level playing field" upon which all can compete on an equal footing, after some limited transitional concessions, is totally fallacious as long as companies, countries, and communities have vastly different strengths, resources, interests, and aims. The fundamental question is: how can a single set of global rules be comprehensive, but fine-tuned and flexible enough to ensure equity, sustainability and stability?

The more fundamental fallacy is that a single set of rules and a single global paradigm can be applied to international economic relations, and to regional, national, or even very local economic entities. Countries, communities, and peoples around the world are located at totally different levels of development and pursue or favor different forms and methods of development. This requires not merely temporary exemptions but different conceptions. This is a broad and complex challenge, and many arguments and organizations (such as the UN socioeconomic agencies) have to be deployed in what is a fundamentally important paradigmatic debate. In this context, however, SDTs can also be utilized, within the WTO itself, as a principle and a precedent from which to argue the case for diverse paths and distinctive models of development.

B. IMPLEMENTATION OF OBLIGATIONS AND INTERROGATIONS

IN RECOGNITION OF THE IMBALANCED NOTED ABOVE, the implementation of WTO rules within national jurisdictions cannot merely be a question of automatic compliance. This should not be a simple one-way technical/legal process. At the very outset, there have to be interrogations as to whether the required compliance with WTO multilateral trade agreements—for example on "national treatment" for global corporations—conforms to established constitutional principles, such as those on preferences and affirmative action commitments by government, and other basic national social and economic aims, political /security needs, and legal provisions.

Even in pursuing such legal analyses, developing countries

face other problems and choices. Given the considerable deficiencies they have in terms of technical resources and legal capacities, compounded by the belated accession of most of them to GATT/WTO, developing countries should directly link their fulfillment of obligations to adequate technical and financial assistance. This has, in fact, already been promised because without such assistance, the system is manifestly not fully inclusive and "global." However, such technical assistance should also be appropriate to fulfill their needs, and not merely consist of training on the WTO by the WTO amounting to little more than instructions on how to implement its rules and regulations.[14] Even the belated High Level Meeting within the WTO in 1998, in supposed fulfillment of these promises, has still not fully dealt with the broader difficulties and more fundamental needs of the LLDCs.

The developing countries are also on strong moral and political grounds in demanding that their implementation of WTO obligations also be directly linked to—and even conditional upon—full implementation of the commitments made to them by the governments of the most developed countries at Marrakesh in 1994. The problem is that, at the legal level, the contractual obligations on the one hand, and the compensatory developed country undertakings on the other, are of a different order. The latter is merely in the "best endeavor" category, which means that it is voluntary and non binding. There are, however, other fully legal and binding commitments by the most developed countries that simply continue to be evaded. This is partly through the use of a range of technical devices, but more fundamentally because the WTO works on the principle that an evasion or abuse only becomes official, once it is challenged in the DSU and proven to be prejudicial to trade interests and rights. Most developing countries simply cannot pursue such processes other than through repeated, but generally ignored, formal political statements and collective declarations. This is particularly the pattern in Africa, with its repeated, but generally futile, collective declarations through the OAU.

Continuing to pose the non compliance of the most developed countries with their own formal undertakings—such as that of the United States in relation to the Agreement on Textiles and Clothing—could also be utilized as an effective tactical weapon by the developing countries in another way. Insistence on prompt and full compliance could be an effective counteraction to covert attempts by some such governments to pose the implementation of their own existing obligations as trade-offs for other countries accepting "new issues" for negotiation. This is highly questionable because the established rights (of developing countries) and existing obligations (of developed countries) must stand in their own right and be implemented as such, without new conditionalities or new *quid pro quo* concessions being required.

C. IMPACT ASSESSMENT AND POSSIBLE MODIFICATIONS

IMPLEMENTATION SHOULD, above all, be linked to and conditional upon intensive and impartial reviews of the substance and imbalanced effects of WTO rules and MTAs. This has to be undertaken with a view to establishing not only their technical feasibility and legal consistency or conformity, but also their basic applicability to developing countries, to their different economic sectors with their respective needs and vulnerabilities. This, in turn, is not simply a question of invoking temporary exceptions and exemptions, but of questioning the very objectives and implications of agreements that most developing countries acceded to only "after the event."

All agreements should be subject to such scrutiny for their "compliance" with the situations and needs of developing countries. They must be closely analyzed for their deficiencies and imbalances, and clear proposals for changes must be required. One such change already being put forward by various developing countries is that, in the interests of domestic industrial development, TRIMs should not bar developing countries from setting local content requirements upon the direct investment ventures of foreign capital in their countries. This is but one example in an extensive range of proposals. Much work has already been done on behalf of developing countries in analysis [Das, 1998; UNCTAD, 1998], and in capacity building especially for LLDCs in Africa [SEATINI-UNDP, 1998, 1999].

Fortunately, there are also programmed opportunities within the WTO that could be used to argue for and obtain modifications and amendments to existing regulations and agreements. Formal provisions have been made for regular reviews of a wide array of issues, including safeguards, technical barriers to trade, rules of origin, dispute settlements, and a whole range of other technical issues. There are also provisions for special reviews of existing agreements on subsidies, anti dumping, services, TRIPs, TRIMs, and others. All of these are part of what is called the built-in agenda, which is clearly very full and technically extremely complicated. In addition to the above reviews, the WTO agenda includes further formal negotiations still due on agriculture, services, rules of origin, and antidumping.

The main problem for developing countries in pursuing their demands through such reviews are, however, not only their lack of adequate technical capacity and personnel, but the overwhelming political weight and proactive initiatives of the most powerful countries in determining the priorities of the WTO agenda. Thus, even as the developing countries struggle to cope with the burdensome built-in agenda inherited from the Uruguay Round, the more developed countries are already promoting a full new round of negotiations to include both existing issues and a range of yet more "new issues."

D. POSSIBLE PRE-EMPTIVE POSITIONS BY DEVELOPING COUNTRIES

OVER AND ABOVE the specific problems within these new issues for their national development priorities and needs, the more fundamental problem is that developing countries are simply not prepared—meaning willing or able—to cope with another full multisectoral round of negotiations while they are still trying to come to grips with the Uruguay Round. If the proposed Millennium Round goes ahead, it will inevitably replicate many of the problematic processes and unbalanced outcomes of the Uruguay Round.

This time, however, developing countries are rather more aware of the nature of the WTO as a negotiating arena in which countries (and corporations) take overt initiatives together and, when necessary, engage in covert collusions to promote their interests against the rest of the world. In these complex and unrelenting battles, legal principles and arguments and social and economic evidence and counter demands must be marshalled by developing countries. However, the WTO is not an assembly of nations or a debating chamber, like the UN. It is a bargaining chamber that, in the final analysis, reflects the balance of economic and political power, as well as tactical skill. In this context, it is essential that developing countries form strategic alliances among themselves where they hold common interests vis-a-vis the hegemonic powers, but still agree on tactical trade-offs on specific issues and interests where they differ among themselves.

There is evidence that bilateral, multilateral, general, specific and overlapping alliances are beginning to be formed among developing countries on the possible content and form of the proposed new round. Such alliances will be extremely important for their strategic engagements and effectiveness, should there be a full new round in the early years of the millennium. However, as in the most effective strategies, the most important first step for the developing countrieswill be to adopt an "advanced bargaining position" from the very outset. In the current situation this means collectively and firmly:

- ◆ opposing any new issues being placed on the WTO agenda until a full review has been made on the impact and implications of existing Uruguay Round and post-Uruguay Round agreements on all developing countries, and especially LLDCs, with appropriate modifications as required

- ◆ opposing any more areas of responsibility and wider coverage, or further powers being attributed to and located within the WTO, until and unless it changes its *modus operandi* and becomes a more fully inclusive, transparent, genuinely impartial and accountable organization and

- ◆ opposing any further full multisectoral round of global negotiations until the current built-in-agenda and programmed negotiations have been carried through, and implemented, and their effects for all economies, in turn, have been verified.

FURTHER AND MORE FUNDAMENTAL AIMS

ALTHOUGH THESE ARE apparently radical positions in the current context of the extremely difficult situation confronting the developing countries, such demands might, at the most, only buy time for them. This could be utilized to deepen their understanding of the many WTO agreements, to work toward much more effective and secure strategic alliances among themselves, to extend public knowledge and engagement on the issues, and to encourage civil society engagement within and across their countries to back up governments in their struggles against the powerful industrialized states. However, given the cautious and even submissive character of most of the governments in the developing countries in relation to the global powers and global institutions, and given the hostility or at least suspicion of most such governments in relation to their own popular organizations, this latter scenario is highly unlikely, if conceived of simply as a strategy led by such governments.

If anything is to be gained from this immediate strategy for "gaining time," it will fundamentally depend upon the full information, effective mobilization, and active engagement of civil society forces within the developing countries in order to simultaneously:

- ◆ bring ever greater pressure to bear on their governments, separately and together, to adopt more principled, proactive, and even challenging positions within the WTO, and in relation to the WTO per se
- ◆ oppose and expose the aims and effects of the WTO agreements upon developing countries and the very nature of the WTO as a highly unsatisfactory "global" institution, and focus this information not (merely) on governments or within the WTO but toward wider public understanding globally, and
- ◆ build up transnational "North-South" as well as "South-South" popular movements and coalitions not only against the WTO agreements and the WTO itself (and related institutions) but against the global neoliberal paradigm that underpins and propels them and that is dividing, destabilizing, and endangering human solidarity and security and planetary sustainability and survival.

1. The former a negotiator on behalf of Egypt in the WTO, and the latter on behalf of India during the Uruguay Round.

2. Very often in the controversial "Green Room" negotiations between the most powerful players that explicitly excluded "outsiders."

3. Although, with the rapid accession of developing countries to GATT during the Uruguay Round, their numbers actually surpassed that of the OECD members when the WTO came to be officially launched in 1995.

4. This is regarded, more generally, as one of the legitimate tactics in litigations.

5. Although many developing countries are not satisfied that this centre, largely due to the interventions of the European Commissioner Leon Brittain, will now not be an independent and separately financed entity—located in Geneva but outside of the WTO—as originally proposed by Norway and some other governments somewhat more sensitive to the disadvantages of the weaker countries.

6. As in Washington's threats of sanctions against countries/ companies not observing U.S. economic measures against Cuba and other countries considered hostile to U.S. interests.

7. As has been argued with respect to the `dumping" of EU agricultural products in developing countries' markets, because the Common Agricultural Programme (CAP) subsidies distort and probably disguise the real costs of production.

8. There is continuing developing country government and global non-governmental opposition to the negotiation of an MIA in the WTO because it is the content and implications of such a "global charter for the TNCs" that is being resisted, and not only the location of such legalization; although the WTO per se as the venue and instrument for such a process is also rejected [*Third World Resurgence*, #95, 1998].

9. As with directors of the Bretton Woods Institutions, the United States and the EU were absolutely adamant that the first director general of the WTO should be a man enjoying their confidence and endorsement.

10. This usage is deliberately employed here to embrace both lesser developing (such as Zimbabwe, or Ghana) and least developed countries (such as Malawi or Mozambique), the latter commonly referred to as LDCs; and is not the same usage that the WTO makes of this term.

11. Which also happens, coincidentally, to be the year in which the effective derogation that the United States enjoys on textiles and clothing comes to an end.

12. The EU has offered full duty free (although not quota-free) access to its markets for all products from all LDCs. This was endorsed at the first WTO Ministerial meeting in Singapore in 1996, but only as an "autonomous," meaning non-obligatory, undertaking by the rest of the WTO members.

13. Based on the direct observation and assessment by this writer who was present at the SMC.

14. This is precisely how the WTO and the International Trade Center are currently interpreting and implementing their technical assistance programs for LLDCs.

REFERENCES

Abugre C. (1998), "The proposed Multilateral Investment Agreement (MIA) and Africa's desire for Foreign Direct Investment," mimeo, paper presented at first meeting of the African Trade Network (ATN), February 1998, Accra, Ghana.

Brenner R. (1998), "The Economics of Global Turbulence" in New Left Review #229, May-June 1998, London.

Clairmont F. (1996), "The Rise and Fall of Economic Liberalism - The Making of the Economic Gulag," Third World Network, Penang, Malaysia.

Das B.L. (1998), "An Introduction to the WTO Agreements" in "Trade and Development Issues and the WTO" series of the Third World Network, Penang, Malaysia.

Das B.L. (1998b) "The WTO Agreements—Deficiencies, Imbalances and Required Changes" in "Trade and Development Issues and the WTO" series of the Third World Network, Penang, Malaysia.

Egypt (1998), "Special and Differential Treatment for Developing Countries in the Multilateral Trading System" Communication from Egypt to the WTO General Council Committee on Trade and Development, WT/GC/109, 5 November, 1998, Geneva.

European Commission (EC) (1995), "Objectives and Contents of the European Commission Initiative for Establishing International Rules for Foreign Investments," Europe Documents, Bulletin Quotidien #1926, 22 March 1995, Brussels

European Union, (1998), "EU/WTO : EU Proposes Increasing Transparency, Professionalism and Effectiveness of the Dispute Settlement System of the World Trade Organization," Bulletin Quotidien #7327, 22 October 1998, Brussels.

India (1998), "Developing Countries seek review of S&D implementation," report on presentation by India to the WTO General Council preparatory process for the 3rd Ministerial meeting, reported in Third World Economics #197, 16-30 November 1998, Penang, Malaysia.

Keet D. (1997), "Integrating the World Community - Political Challenges and Opportunities for Developing Countries" in Southern African Perspectives #70, Center for Southern African Stduies, School of Government, University of the Western Cape.

Keet D. (1998), "Anticipating and Influencing the WTO Review of Regional Trade Agreements (RTAs)," paper presented at the "Southern and Eastern African Trade Information and Negotiations Initiative (SEATINI) workshop for African Trade Officials and Negotiators towards the Second WTO Ministerial Meeting and Future Negotiations" mimeo, 29 March—4 April 1998, Harare, Zimbabwe.

Keet D. (1999), "Regional Integration and Development in Southern Africa— the Implications of a Reciprocal Free Trade Agreement within the EU," in "Farewell to Lome?—The Impact of Neo-Liberal EU Policies on the ACP Countries," Venro Campaign, German EU Presidency, Koordination Sudliches Afrika, Bonn, 1999.

Khor M. (1996), "The WTO and the Proposed Multilateral Investment Agreement: Implications for Developing Countries and Proposed Positions," TWN Trade and Development Series #2, Penang, Malaysia

Khor M. (1997), "Competing Views on "Competition Policy" in the WTO," mimeo, paper presented at the Southern and East African Trade Information and Negotiating Initiative, Harare, April 1997

Khor M. (1999), "New non-trade issues in the WTO - a comment," in Third World Resurgence #108, August 1999, Penang, Malaysia.

Onimode B. (1992), "A future for Africa—beyond the politics of adjustment," Earthscan in association with the Institute for African Alternatives, London

Organization of African Unity (OAU) (1998), "Declaration of the African Countries on the High Level Meeting on Integrated Initiatives for Least Developed Countries' Trade Development," OAU/AEC/TRD/MIN/EXP(1), 6-9 April, 1998, Harare, Zimbabwe.

OXFAM (1998), "For Richer, and for Poorer? Development Challenges for the WTO," briefing paper prepared for the WTO Ministerial and 50th Anniversary Celebrations in Geneva, May 1998, Oxford.

Ragavan C. (1990), "Recolonization—GATT, the Uruguay Round and the Third World," Third World Network, Penang, Malaysia.

Shahin M. (1996), "From Marrakesh to Singapore: The WTO and Developing Countries," Third World Network, Penang, Malaysia.

Southern and Eastern African Trade Information and Negotiations Initiative (SEATINI) workshop in conjunction with the United Nations Development Programme (UNDP) for African Trade Officials and Negotiators towards the Second WTO Ministerial Meeting and Future Negotiations, 29 March—4 April 1998, Harare, Zimbabwe.

Third World Resurgence (1998), "NGOs reject any proposal for moving the MAI or an investment agreement to the WTO," reproduced in Third World Resurgence #95, July 1998, Penang, Malaysia

United Nations Conference on Trade and Development (UNCTAD) (1998), "Special and Differential Treatment: Search for a New Strategy," Discussion Paper prepared by UNCTAD Secretariat for the Regional Programme for Capacity Building in Trade and Development for Africa, Geneva.

UNCTAD (1998b), "Developing a positive trade negotiating agenda: issues of interest to Africa," discussion paper prepared by UNCTAD secretariat, ibid.

World Bank (1991), "Intra-regional Trade in Sub-Saharan Africa," World Bank Economic and Finance Divisions, Africa Region, May 1991, Washington.

World Trade Organization (WTO) (1996), "Report to the First WTO Ministerial Conference," 9-13 December 1996, Singapore.

TWO CASES OF
CORPORATE RULE

The following two articles were originally delivered as speeches at the International Forum on Globalization's conference on Corporate Rule in Toronto, Canada, April 1998. Sara Larrain of Chile and Oronto Douglas of Nigeria each describe the quite different ways that transnational corporations have gained nearly total control of both economic and political processes within their respective countries. While neither directly implicates the World Trade Organization—the particular focus of this book—both examples express the inherent consequences of a global economic system that gives first priority to corporations over all other considerations, from human rights and democracy to the environment. In Chile, says Larrain, the conversion to a corporate-led export economy was the main way that Augosto Pinochet gained a level of acceptance and engagement with the international community. Trade liberalization was his ticket to respectability, but at great cost not only to human rights, but also to the environment and social welfare. Larrain laments that the advent of a democratically elected president has actually done very little to slow the harms of this neoliberal conversion.

In Nigeria, as Oronto Douglas describes, corporate rule has been very direct and concrete: Oil development and export are given top priority, while also bringing on dictatorship, environmental devastation, assaults on tribal cultures, and mass slaughter.

THE CASE OF CHILE: DICTATORSHIP AND NEOLIBERALISM

Sara Larrain

Sarah Larrain is a former professor at the Catholic University of Chile, and is the coordinator of the Chilean Ecological Action Network. She is also co-founder of a new Chilean political party, the Partido Alternative de Cambio, and stood for the presidency of Chile in the 1999 elections. She was the principal author of a study, Sustainable Chile, *that became the platform for her election campaign.*

SOME OF YOU PROBABLY KNOW the history of my country during the last 25 years. The bloody coup in Chile in 1973 put in place a military government that was not trained to govern or administrate a country. Thus, it handed over these responsibilities to the business community, which, of course, had supported the coup. Following the guidance of corporations, the Chilean government began to redesign laws governing the economy and society. In addition, they began to redesign our constitution. The one they adopted in 1980 allowed corporations wide-ranging freedoms, based on the argument that this would lead to economic growth and political stability.

Another motivation for opening up the economy to foreign investment and for promoting exports was to try to regain international acceptance. After the coup, Chile was shunned by much of the international community because of the widespread human rights violations carried out by the junta.

Over time, Chile did indeed become the "Latin American tiger," with economic growth of 6 to 7 percent annually during the last 13 years. However, the competitiveness of the Chilean economy was based on natural resource exports, low wages, and unequal wealth distribution. I will present the case of forests and mining to show how the rewrite of the legal system impacted natural resources. Secondly, I will discuss very briefly the change of the labor law, as a second key instrument in the redesign of the Chilean economy.

The military government changed both the mining code and the water code to attract foreign investment. One of these changes, Decree 600, stimulated large investments at the expense of the local communities and allowed companies to obtain water rights. These have led to a reduction in agricultural activities in some communities; many small farmers have been forced to abandon their lands.

To promote exports in the forest sector, the government introduced legislation like Decree 701, which subsidized between 75 to 90 percent of forest company costs, and freed the companies from taxes. This mechanism encouraged the big companies to substitute native forest with pine and eucalyptus and channeled 96 percent of the subsidies to the big farmers; only 4 percent has gone to small farmers.

As a result of these policies, Chilean exports in forest products increased 1,600 percent. According to our Central Bank, if present forest policies remain, native forests in Chile could disappear by the year 2025.

Similar policies to encourage increased exports have been imposed in the fishery and agricultural sectors. Today 90 percent of my country's exports are natural resource products. To give a picture of the pressure this places on the environment, it's important to know that just 10 natural resource products make up 64 percent of Chilean exports. So the pressure on the environment is very focused, and of course it is this exploitation of our environment that has fueled our high economic growth rate.

This high growth rate has also had tremendous social costs. Our poverty rate grew from 20 percent of the population in 1970 to 40 percent in 1985. Today, after 13 years of 6 to 7 percent annual growth, almost 30 percent of the Chilean population (about 4 million people) still struggles at the poverty level. And poverty today is not because of the lack of jobs, since the unemployment rate is only 5 to 6 percent. The poor have jobs, but they have very low-paying jobs.

It's very clear that economic growth in Chile has been subsidized by low wages. This is continuing even now because after seven years of a transition to democracy, we are burdened with the same labor laws as were set in place by the companies during the dictatorship. Workers have no right to collective bargaining or to fight for higher pay. The final result is a very unequal distribution of income. Some 10 percent of Chile's population earn about 60 percent of the income, while the poorest 10 percent obtain only 1.7 percent. Sadly, in this kind of neoliberal export-oriented economic model, the income distribution is bad whether it's run by a dictatorship or a democracy. The income gap has continued to get worse during the period 1994 to 1996.

In conclusion, I need to say that my country is still making legislative changes designed to further promote our global competitiveness at the expense of the environment and society as a whole. For example, they are continuing to privatize the health system and the social funds, including the pension funds. This means that all areas in the country need to function as corporate departments, thus generating profits in all the different economic sectors. So the real problem here is that we have developed a corporate state with no concept of a social contract, and this doesn't really change with democracy. Trade liberalization, the free market, and the free society—these are all about having access to Coca-Cola, but not access to wealth, pensions, health care, or education. This is the case of Chile, and I think that many countries have their own similar story, with different characteristics but the same process.

THE CASE OF NIGERIA: CORPORATE OIL AND TRIBAL BLOOD

Oronto Douglas

Oronto Douglas is a leading human rights attorney in Nigeria, and served as one of the lawyers on the defense team for the Ogoni leader Ken Saro Wiwa, later executed by Nigeria's military rulers. Douglas is also founder and deputy director of Environmental Rights Action. Though he has been arrested and tortured by the military regime, he continues to work for and speak out on issues of social justice in a corporate military state.

THE POLITICAL MECHANISMS of corporate rule in the geographical area called Nigeria can only be understood from a historical perspective. This is one country that was designed by corporations for corporations and simply disregards the people who live there. And so to understand it, we have to look at the past.

First we have to look at slavery. As many as 10 million people from West Africa were shipped to America to fulfill one common condition, the condition of ensuring that labor is constantly supplied; the use of the human being to sustain factories and other economic activities in the Americas. Then, of course, that phase passed when they discovered that the slaves were reproducing. And, of course, the world was beginning to take note of the indignity that slavery had imposed on fellow human beings. The practice had to change to colonialism.

Active colonialism was then followed in the area of black South Africa, where Africa had reigned supreme, and then in other countries. In the present era, it has been *new* colonialism, that in my country has been manifested via a military dictatorship that is in service to this new colonialism, which basically is directed, controlled and pushed upon us by transnational corporations. So if we look at our current situation from that perspective, you can then understand where we are coming from.

Imperial Britain was actually very unwilling to colonize Nigeria. Records show that Lord Salisbury, for instance, described Nigeria as a "malaria swamp," and said he would not want in any way to have anything to do with that area. But multinational corporations then pushed the government of Britain to take active control in order to compete with France. We do know that in 1885 and 1886, the European powers, armed only with pencils and erasers, cut Africa into boxes and squares, so much so that when you look at a map of Africa, what you see is not natural borders, but countries of boxes and squares. So the companies and corporations had to send people like Mongo Park, the Landau brothers and the imperialist soldier called Lord Lugat, to take active charge in that potentially rich new country called Nigeria. All these actions were inspired by greed.

In 1895, the United African Company was in direct confrontation with local people over a natural resource called palm oil, which was needed in Europe to produce butter and other types of creams. The local people from the central part of the Niger Delta felt that they were being exploited and challenged by the United African Company. Things escalated so that the people attacked the company's trading post and destroyed the instruments of trade, like the drums and containers. When the United African Company reported that some local savages had invaded their trading post, Britain retaliated by bringing in naval forces. The town of Nembe was bombed, killing over 4,000 people, mostly women and children. The men ran away, leaving the women and the children to bear the brunt of the invading British naval forces. But take note that it was the multinational corporations that directed and controlled the British government to take those reprisal actions against a local community.

The same thing was replayed in 1897 when Benin City, a very famous kingdom, was invaded, works of art stolen, and all with the goal of capturing the rich forest resources of the Benin area.

And then, of course, in 1937, the well-known monstrous multinational called Shell emerged on the scene. It arrived in Nigeria in 1937. By 1956, it discovered crude oil in commercial quantities in the central part of the Niger Delta. By 1958, Ogoni people from the Boma oil fields had produced tremendous quantities of oil; the same happened in Andoni, Urhoba, Itsekiri, and so on.

But it was not until 1967 that the cruel hands of the multinationals became apparent. Most people in Europe and America think that the war that broke out in Nigeria in 1967 was an ethnic war, but it was not. It was an oil war, engineered by the multinationals. If you look closely at the history, the Ebus of the eastern region were crying out against the persecution of the Lothin region. And, of course, the east thought that they could survive because of the numerous oil reserves there. And so they decided to secede. But secession would have meant that the oil that was then under the control of Shell (and to a large extent of Britain), would have moved away from British control. So, Shell moved swiftly to advise the British government never to back secession. The government's subsequent actions led to a civil war in which over one million people died between 1967 and 1970.

And so it is clear that all strategy toward the capture of political power in Nigeria is strategy aimed and directed at the capture of oil wells. It is important that we keep that in the back of our minds as we look at Nigeria.

Directly from the time when Nigeria was created by corporations, the oil multinationals have been involved. We have seen documents that they were actually involved in the fashioning of an independent constitution for us. Most of the rulers in Nigeria are people who have either been directors or members of the boards of multinationals, principally Shell. Shell has fashioned a new vision, what they call Vision 2010, a vision they have sold to the military dictatorship of General Abacha. And they have also reportedly been heavily involved in the importation of weapons and arms. They retain their own police force, and through their immense power they have plundered a lot of places. In the late 1980s and early 1990s, several communities were rendered obsolete.

Then from 1993 to 1995, the Ogoni land was turned into a killing field rather than a drilling field. Even if it is a drilling field, it has been the drilling of death and the complete massacre of a defenseless people.

If you think that evil is coming only from the West, it is not true in the case of Nigeria. When people argue, for example, for a South-South cooperation, some of us who have been involved, who are in the front line, take it with a pinch of salt, because, of late, we do know that companies from China, and from elsewhere in Asia, have taken positions of plunder. Recently, the Western Metal Product Company, a Hong Kong-based multinational, was involved in the plunder of Omo Forest in Western Nigeria, and is now strategically positioned to exploit the biggest forest estate in Cross River, in the west-southeastern part of Nigeria.

We believe that if we are going to resolve all these issues we have to challenge the multinationals very vigorously. Our anger must be focused on a complete dismantling of the authorities of corporate rule. Because they have not only caused social disintegration of our culture and our tradition, they have led to the introduction of foreign diseases and the destruction of our cultural ethos. They have led to the destabilization of our mainstream economy and livelihoods. We are basically agrarian people, dependent on fishing and farming; we do not have the technology that the West or other parts of the world have. But we have peace, we have laws, and we intend to promote this.

So from palm oil in 1895, to the crude oil of the present day, when Ken Saro Wiwa and so many Ogonis were killed, we have faced very monstrous multinationals geared toward the destruction of our very existence. It is not only Shell. Chevron, Mobil, AGIP, and all the other multinationals that have recently emerged from Asia and China are involved in the complete desecration of our very dignity as human beings.

THE SOUTH IN THE NORTH

Anuradha Mittal

Policy Director, Food First—Institute for Food and Development Policy

THE PAPERS IN THIS BOOK have presented an excellent case against the global economy. They show how for most of the Third World, trade liberalization has come to connote colonialism and a dominating world capitalist system. The papers explain the total denial of rights to those who live on the peripheries of the global nation-states system—rights to common property, rights of indigenous communities in their homelands, rights of slum-dwellers to homes, rights of peasants to land, seeds and the ecological genepool. They show how the unregulated flow of global capital has placed the fate of developing economies at the mercy of Wall Street traders. What I would like to add at the end of this collection is the point that the nations of the global South are not the only victims of this process. There is also a "South" in the North—right here in the United States, that is being severely harmed by economic globalization.

◆ ◆ ◆

"It isn't that I never worked," said Katherine Engels, "I've worked since I was 14 years old." Engels, a grandmother and president of the Kensington Welfare Rights Union, was testifying at a congressional hearing on the human rights implications of increasing hunger, poverty, and economic insecurity in America. "With the jobs that are out there you're not making enough to live. When you're hungry, it's really hard. Sometimes I psyche myself up to a cup of tea and try to make myself feel as though I just ate a full course meal, even though I didn't. Sometimes I roll bread up into little dough balls to try fill myself up. Mothers go hungry at night so their children can eat. You have to find a way to feed your kids no matter what it takes. And if it takes going in people's trash cans, hey, I have no pride when it comes to my kids."

A triumphant view dominates media coverage of the U.S. economy: the lowest yearly unemployment rate in a quarter century, rising profits, a balanced budget, and declining numbers of Americans classified as poor. While all this may be good, Katherine Engels knows that the problem is bigger then her personal struggle. There is nothing new about poverty in America. But never before have poor families like the Engels had to wage their daily struggles amid such pervasive chatter about unprecedented prosperity. The present economic optimism masks the deepening erosion of the American dream for millions in this country.

Economic globalization promoted through trade agreements such as the General Agreement on Tariffs and Trade (GATT), North American Free Trade Agreement (NAFTA) and the World Trade Organization (WTO) is changing the face of the country. In the globalizing world people are confronting new threats to human security. In both poor and rich countries, dislocations from economic and corporate restructuring, and from dismantling the institutions of social protection, have meant greater insecurity in jobs and incomes. The pressures of global competition have led countries and employers to adopt more flexible labor policies with more precarious work arrangements and lax environmental laws. Mergers and acquisitions have come with corporate restructuring and have sped up massive lay offs. The United States is no exception.

In the age of economic globalization we live in a world which has become a single economic zone tied together by corporate production networks literally spanning the globe. The real beneficiaries of this trend are not countries but big transnational corporations that can produce and sell goods as well as offer services anywhere in the global marketplace.

As corporations travel the world looking for the most favorable conditions—the lower costs, the fewest regulations, the most compliant labor—it gives them a powerful advantage over those who need to make a daily living. In the global economy, local, regional, and national governments must compete with international counterparts to encourage transnational employers to set up shop in their communities or to keep plants from leaving. The result has been a rush to the bottom; a downward spiral of wages and living conditions as nations and corporations discipline their labor forces for global market shares. Working people everywhere are being forced to pay a disproportionate share of the burden of globalization.

Making matters worse, deindustrialization—the decline of manufacturing industries—is doing its part to deplete the productive base of the developed countries. Instead of plowing profits back into existing plants or investing in new manufacturing operations to spur innovation, upgrade equipment and workers skills, many corporations have become runaways. This has had a profoundly negative impact on the economic security of the workers and communities as they lose control over their economic futures.

This trend is not confined to the U.S. alone. Corporations are now footloose. Workers in developing countries have no job security. Other low-wage sites threaten them, just as they threaten U.S. workers. Since 1973, the income gap between rich and poor nations has grown from 44 to 1 to 72 to 1. The gap between rich and poor within most countries has grown rapidly as well, followed closely by deepening social problems. This is rampant in America as well, where we have seen increased poverty and homelessness, even in times of economic prosperity. Behind this alarming picture lie structural changes in the global economy brought about by rapid increases in trade and capital flows. Trade agreements have not only accelerated in a globalizing economy but have created a globalized South. The world is becoming one—characterized by increasing income inequalities, poverty and hunger.

BOOMING ECONOMY WITH GROWING POVERTY; THE "THIRD WORLDIZATION" OF AMERICA

IN THE MEDIA and in the speeches of national leaders, Americans are often presented with an official portrait of America's progress. This portrait typically includes the Gross Domestic Product, the stock market, the Index of leading Economic Indicators, the balance of trade, the inflation rate, and other similar measures. These figures and measures mold our perception of the state of the nation and provide a false answer to the question: "How are we doing?" and "Can we attribute this growth to the free market policies?"

In order to know the true state of our union, we need to explore other measurements. These include the well-being of America's children, the accessibility of health care, the quality of education, the adequacy of housing, the security and satisfaction of work, adequate access to food for all, and the nation's sense of community and diversity. Only when we have a complete view of the nation's progress, can we answer how America is doing and what issues we need to address.

The true effects of global corporatization on working people can be seen in the damage that has already been wreaked upon Americans, which has paralleled the destruction of livelihoods, environment and agriculture in the southern economies. It is now well documented that NAFTA has hurt workers in all these countries. The U.S. Economic Policy Institute has estimated that NAFTA eliminated some 600,000 U.S. jobs during its first two-and-a-half years. During the same period, the new jobs created within the United States were mostly in the lower-paying sectors of the U.S. economy. According to its more recent estimates, the manufacturing sector has lost 272,000 jobs since March 1998. The hardest-hit industries include textiles and apparel (90,000 jobs lost), electronic equipment and components (88,000), industrial machinery, including machine tools and construction equipment (54,000), and iron and steel blast furnaces (8,000 jobs lost since June, 1998 alone). Five thousand aerospace jobs were lost in January 1999, reflecting a 20 percent surge in airplane parts imports in 1998. Technological innovation and anti-labor government policies have caused some of the job loss, but economic globalization is the driving force.

Another trend evident in this new economy is that the workplace is now highly volatile and characterized by high levels of job insecurity. A study done by San Jose-based Working Partnerships USA and the Economic Policy Institute, Washington-based think tank, shows that only 21 percent of California workers have been in their jobs for more than 10 years. For example, high tech companies tend to use high numbers of contract and temporary workers to do a specific project. This new economy is also characterized by widening income and benefits gap between those with high skills and those in lower-end service jobs.

In the meanwhile, the U.S. job losses due to NAFTA continued to increase in 1998. The U.S. Department of Labor certified that 216,156 workers have lost their jobs because of either shifts in production to Mexico or Canada or because of increased imports from those countries. These kind of closures and lay offs have ignited workers response to trade agreements around the country. For example, it prompted United Steel Workers of America to challenge the constitutionality of NAFTA in May 1999. According to the USWA President, George Becker, "We want NAFTA scrapped and look forward to presenting our arguments on why NAFTA must be viewed as a treaty. Our government has never explained to the hundreds of thousands of workers and their families across America who have lost their livelihood, how NAFTA is an executive agreement and not a treaty."

Along with this disturbing trend, the country's merchandise trade deficit rose 25 percent in 1998, its highest level on record. The aggregate U.S. trade deficit in goods hit a staggering $248 billion in 1998. The International Monetary Fund recently estimated that the U.S. current account deficit, the broadest measure of the U.S. trade balance, will increase by an additional $57 billion, or 25 percent in 1999. Rising trade deficits have already taken a toll on the manufacturing sector which continues to suffer in 1999 as the trade gap widens.

What is the human dimension of this economic globalization? Despite glowing media reports on our booming economy, an estimated 46 million Americans, nearly 17 percent of the population, live below the poverty line. New data released by the USDA in its report on Household Food Security in the United States, 1995–1998, suggests that despite the strength of the national economy, hunger remains a serious problems for a sizeable number of Americans. In 1998, approximately 36 million people in 10.5 million households across the country did not have adequate access to food. About 20 percent of all children under the age of 18 (or 14 million children) lived in food insecure homes where food may have been scarce. United States

Agricultural Secretary, Dan Glickman, was reported as saying, "During this, the most prosperous economy in decades, it should shock most Americans to learn that hunger persists and it is in every state. The problem of hunger amid America's plenty cannot be ignored."

The Children's Defense Fund (CDF) released a report in August 1999 which documents that the number of children living at or below one-half of the poverty line increased by 426,000 between 1996 and 1997. Today one in five children under five lives in poverty—the highest rate among industrialized countries. As many as 7 million Americans are homeless. In just one city, San Francisco, health department figures show that a record 157 people died on the streets in 1998. Their deaths were attributed to the lack of shelter beds and affordable housing.

The number of Americans who lack health insurance continued to increase, climbing to 44.3 million in spite of a prosperous economy. The ranks of the uninsured grew by about 1 million in 1998, according to the figures released by the Census Bureau, and the proportion of those without coverage is still one in six.

Economic globalization has only widened the after-tax income gaps between those with the highest incomes and other Americans and is projected to reach their widest point in 1999. The top 2.7 million people have as much income as the bottom 100 million. In other words, the richest 1 percent of Americans is projected to have as much after-income in 1999 as the 38 percent of Americans with the lowest incomes. Wealth is even more concentrated at the top than at any time since the Depression, with the wealthiest 1 percent of households owning nearly 40 percent of the nation's wealth. The bottom 80 percent of households own just 16 percent of the nation's wealth, less than half of what the wealthiest one percent of the population possessed.

While the wealthy grow steadily richer, riding the stock market surges, millions of working Americans grope for their infinitesimal share of the boom. Many are victims of layoffs or lack the skills now in demand; many have been forced off welfare as part of nationwide reforms. Wages often are too meager to allow self-sufficiency; work is grueling or mind-numbing, on night shifts, without health insurance or other benefits.

It doesn't have to be that way, in a nation like ours. The wealth and resources clearly exist for every man, woman and child to have a roof over their head and food in their belly, and for them to have access to a decent education, health care and a job that pays a living wage. The sad truth is that blind pursuance of the market has created an economy that puts corporate profits before people's lives, that places economic efficiency over opportunity and compassion for all.

CALL TO ACTION!
FLESHING OUT THE ALTERNATIVE

TRADE IS ONE of the most important issues that defines the end of this millennium and the start of the next one. Today the framework for free trade is being set in international law while the transnational corporations use their financial and political muscle to usher in an intense period of trade liberalization.

Markets are not the first nor the last word in human development. Many essentials for human development are provided outside the market, but these are being destroyed and squeezed by the pressures of the global competition. When the market dominates social and political outcomes, the rewards of globalization spread unequally. When the market gets out of hand, the instabilities show up in the boom or bust cycles as evident in the Asian financial crisis. When the profit motive of the market gets out of hand, it sacrifices respect for justice and human rights.

The time has come to step back from this mania for free

trade at any cost, assess the damage, and seek a new start. The goal is not to stop international trade. In appropriate circumstances and under the right conditions, international trade can support local economic development, provide needed goods that cannot be produced domestically, and create jobs. But trade bills and treaties designed to favor the wealthiest and most powerful corporations at the expense of everyone else are wrong. Recognizing the potential of trade, there is a need for a set of principles to serve as the basis for a different kind of trade policy, one under which the benefits of trade might flow primarily to the countries and communities most in need. What they add up to is selective or negotiated integration into the global economy, as opposed to indiscriminate globalization and trade liberalization.

PRINCIPLES TO BE MET
BY ANY TRADE BILL, TREATY OR POLICY

* *Unconditional Debt Cancellation:* The principal reason many governments in Southern developing countries are capital-starved is because of the unsustainable burden placed on them by debt service. Total annual debt payments are currently higher than the sum of all foreign investment, plus all foreign aid. While free trade is often promoted as a way to get foreign investment capital into poor economies, debt cancellation is the single most important short-term way to inject needed capital into developing countries economies.
  A centerpiece of any trade-related (or aid-related) bill or policy relating to the Third World must be unconditional debt cancellation. Debt cancellation must not be made conditional upon countries modifying any of their own economic policies or laws, including making them accept structural adjustment or market-opening requirements.

- *True Participatory Process:* The development of future trade bills or policies must occur through a participatory process with broad representation of "affected" civil society in the U.S. and abroad. Time and again trade policies have been developed and implemented without the participation of those who stand to be most negatively affected. These include farmers and small businesses in developing countries who must compete with a flood of cheap imports, and workers here in America who may lose their jobs as factories move to countries with cheap labor.

- *No Corporate Welfare:* There should be no direct or indirect subsidies, or favored status for transnational corporations (TNCs) included in the bill/policy. That means no export credits or guarantees may be included that help TNCs penetrate Southern/developing country economies to the detriment of local businesses.

- *No Coercion:* "Poorer" countries should not be coerced through conditions or threatened by exclusion into removing their own tariff and non-tariff trade barriers, nor weakening the fiscal, trade-related and other policy instruments at their disposal for guiding domestic economic development.

- *Sovereignty Over Basic Economic Policy:* All countries must retain the right to establish currency and import controls, set the conditions of trade and investment to meet the needs of their people, and control flows of capital and resources into/out of the country as a legitimate means to achieve domestic economic stability.

- *No Food Dumping:* There should be no dumping of foodstuffs disguised as "trade liberalization." Each country has a right to protect basic food production as it sees fit. Cheap imports undercut the ability of local farmers to stay in business, often driving them off the land and into cities. This undercuts long-term national food security and creates dependence on imports. Self-reliance in basic necessities gives countries and communities a stronger bargaining position in the global economy.

◆ *Only Small and Medium Businesses:* Favored trade status should only be granted to: a) 100 percent domestically-owned small and medium size enterprises abroad, and b) small and medium enterprises (especially 100 percent minority owned) in the U.S.

◆ *Close Loopholes:* Provision must be made to close the "sub-contracting" loopholes and transfer pricing by which TNCs use locally-owned sub-contractors to intentionally evade taxes and national ownership, minimum wage, workplace safety and trade regulations.

◆ *Mandatory Impact Assessment:* There must be an independent and objective social/economic/cultural/environmental impact assessment prepared with full participation and partnership with the public and civil society organizations (with on-going monitoring thereafter), and strong provisions for canceling part or all of the proposed bill/policy if negative impacts are likely or occur during implementation.

◆ *Subordinate to Human Rights and National Constitutions:* There must be clear, binding language that gives legal precedence over trade agreements to each country's domestic constitutional provisions, as well as to international conventions and treaties on human rights and the environment.

◆ *Large Compensation Fund:* A substantial fund should be created to compensate regions and peoples negatively affected by changes in trade and development patterns brought about by the bill or policy. An example is how some regions in Europe that were hurt by integration into the European Economic Community (EEC) received special subsidies from the European Union.

◆ *Human Beings Have More Rights Than Goods and Capital:* When a "common market free trade zone" is created (like the EEC or NAFTA), labor must be given the same mobility as capital and goods (as it was in the EEC, but was not in NAFTA). Otherwise excessive downward pressure is exerted on wages (as in NAFTA). Money and goods should not be favored over people.

◆ *No Divide and Conquer:* One country or region should never be "played off against another" (i.e., do not take import quotas from Latin America to give to Africa, etc.).

These principles may sound tough and utopian. Some may say that with these criteria, no trade bill would be passed and no treaty signed. Our answer is that no new trade legislation, and no new trade treaties, or the rollback of existing treaties, would be far better than ones which have massively set back human welfare and the environment.

Today's globalization is driven by market expansion—opening national borders to trade, capital, and information. More progress has been made in norms, standards, policies and institutions for open global markets than for people and their rights. The growing interdependence of people's lives around the globe calls for shared commitment to the human development of all people. It is the universalizing logic of labor solidarity, international community, social and economic equity and ecological sustainability that will confront the destructive economic globalization. And a new commitment will emerge, grounded in the ethics of universalism set out in the *Universal Declaration of Human Rights*.

REFERENCES

"Extreme Child Poverty Rises Sharply in 1997," The Children's Defense Fund, Washington DC, August 22, 1999.

"Food First Trade Principles," Backgrounder, Food First/Institute for Food and Development Policy, Fall 1999.

Goldstein, A., "More Americans Lack Medical Coverage," The San Francisco Chronicle, Oct. 4, 1999.

McLeod, R., "Job Boom Brings Insecurity," San Francisco Chronicle, May 25, 1999.

"Measuring Food Security in the United States: Household Food Security in the United States 1995–1998" (Advance Report), United States Department of Agriculture, July 1999.

"New Welfare and Medicaid Bill Bad for Children," Children's Defense Fund Reports, 1996, Vol. 17, No. 7/8

"10% of U.S. Households Found to go Hungry, at Least Part of the Time," San Francisco Chronicle, October 15, 1999.

"The Widening Income Gulf," Center on Budget and Policy Priorities, Washington, DC, September 199.

"Trade Deficits, Job Losses Increase Through 1998," Trade fax, EPI, Washington, DC February 19, 1999.

Uchitelle, L., "Devising New Math to Define Poverty," The New York Times, October 18, 1999.

Index

T

FOOD FIRST BOOKS
OF RELATED INTEREST

The Paradox of Plenty: Hunger in a Bountiful World
Edited by Douglas H. Boucher

Excerpts from Food First's best writings on world hunger and what we can do to change it.   Paperback, $18.95

Basta! Land and the Zapatista Rebellion in Chiapas
Revised edition
George A. Collier with Elizabeth Lowery Quaratiello
Foreword by Peter Rosset

The classic on the Zapatista in a new revised edition, including a preface by Roldolfo Stavenhagen, a new epilogue about the present challenges to the indigenous movement in Chiapas, and an updated bibliography.   Paperback, $14.95

Benedita da Silva: An Afro-Brazilian Woman's Story of Politics and Love
As told to Medea Benjamin and Maisa Mendonça
Foreword by Jesse Jackson

Afro-Brazilian Senator Benedita da Silva shares the inspiring story of her life as an advocate for the rights of women and the poor.   Paperback, $15.95

Dark Victory: The U.S. and Global Poverty
Walden Bello, with Shea Cunningham and Bill Rau
Second edition, with a new epilogue by the author

Offers an understanding of why poverty has deepened in many countries, and analyzes the impact of U.S. economic policies.   Paperback, $14.95

Dragons in Distress: Asia's Miracle Economies in Crisis
Walden Bello and Stephanie Rosenfeld

After three decades of rapid growth, the economies of South Korea, Taiwan, and Singapore are in crisis. The authors offer policy recommendations to break these countries from their unhealthy dependence on Japan and the U.S.   Paperback, $12.95

A Quiet Violence: View from a Bangladesh Village
Betsy Hartmann and James Boyce

The root causes of hunger emerge through the stories of both village landowners and peasants who live at the margin of survival.   Paperback, $17.95

Video: *The Greening of Cuba*
Directed by Jaime Kibben

Cuba has combined time-tested traditional methods with cutting edge bio-technology, reminding us that developed and developing nations can choose a healthier environment and still feed their people.   VHS videotape, $29.95.

Write or call our distributor to place book orders. All orders must be pre-paid. Please add $4.50 for the first book and $1.50 for each additional book for shipping and handling.

LPC Group
1436 West Randolph Street
Chicago, IL 60607
(800) 243-0138
www.coolbooks.com

INTERNATIONAL FORUM
ON GLOBALIZATION

The International Forum on Globalization (IFG) is a research and educational institution comprised of 60 researchers, activists, scholars, and economists, from over 25 countries that seeks to stimulate new thinking and public activity in response to the rapidly emerging economic and political arrangement called the global economy. For over half a decade, the organization has convened some of the world's leading critics of corporate-led economic globalization. The IFG presents seminars, teach-ins, publications, and publishes ads on the social, political, cultural, and environmental effects of globalization. Recent teach-ins have been held in Seattle on the World Trade Organization and in Washington, D.C. on the International Monetary Fund and the World Bank, discussing the power and impact of these institutions on democracy, communities, local economies, and the environment.

The IFG also has special committees and programs on agriculture and food safety; emerging corporate governance; globalization and the environment; alternatives to the new global economy; technology and globalization; and finance and investment.

HOW TO BECOME A MEMBER OF THE IFG

The IFG depends on private contributions and membership gifts in order to sustain its programs and publications. Your support helps to ensure that the negative effects of globalization on culture, human welfare, jobs, democracy, social equality and justice, and the natural world continue to be vigorously brought forward to policymakers, the media, and the general public. Become a member of the IFG and receive benefits such as newsletters, bulletins, and discounts on publications and events. Please contact the IFG for further information on membership levels and accompanying benefits. All donations are tax-deductible.

INTERNATIONAL FORUM ON GLOBALIZATION

1062 Fort Cronkhite   Sausalito, CA 94965

(tel) 415-229-9350   (fax) 415-229-9340   www.ifg.org

ABOUT FOOD FIRST

(Institute for Food and Development Policy)

Food First, also known as the Institute for Food and Development Policy, is a nonprofit research and education-for-action center dedicated to investigating and exposing the root causes of hunger in a world of plenty. It was founded in 1975 by Frances Moore Lappé, author of the bestseller *Diet for a Small Planet*, and food policy analyst Dr. Joseph Collins. Food First research has revealed that hunger is created by concentrated economic and political power, not by scarcity. Resources and decision-making are in the hands of a wealthy few, depriving the majority of land, jobs, and therefore food.

Hailed by *The New York Times* as "one of the most established food think tanks in the country," Food First has grown to profoundly shape the debate about hunger and development.

But Food First is more than a think tank. Through books, reports, videos, media appearances, and speaking engagements, Food First experts not only reveal the often hidden roots of hunger, they show how individuals can get involved in bringing an end to the problem. Food First inspires action by bringing to light the courageous efforts of people around the world who are creating farming and food systems that truly meet people's needs.

HOW TO BECOME A MEMBER OR INTERN OF FOOD FIRST

BECOME A MEMBER OF FOOD FIRST

Private contributions and membership gifts form the financial base of Food First/Institute for Food and Development Policy. The success of the Institute's programs depends not only on its dedicated volunteers and staff, but on financial activists as well. Each member strengthens Food First's efforts to change a hungry world. We invite you to join Food First. As a member you will receive a twenty percent discount on all Food First books. You will also receive our quarterly publication, *Food First News and Views,* and timely *Backgrounders* that provide information and suggestions for action on current food and hunger crises in the United States and around the world. If you want so subscribe to our internet newsletter, *Food Rights Watch,* send us an e-mail at foodfirst@foodfirst.org. All contributions are tax-deductible.

BECOME AN INTERN FOR FOOD FIRST

There are opportunities for interns in research, advocacy, campaigning, publishing, computers, media, and publicity at Food First. Our interns come from around the world. They are a vital part of our organization and make our work possible.

To become a member or apply to become an intern, just call, visit our web site, or clip and return the attached coupon to:

Food First/Institute for Food and Development Policy
398 60th Street, Oakland, CA 94618, USA
Phone: (510) 654-4400 Fax: (510) 654-4551
E-mail: foodfirst@foodfirst.org
Web site: www.foodfirst.org

You are also invited to give a gift membership to others interested in the fight to end hunger.

FOOD FIRST GIFT BOOKS

Please send a Gift Book to (order form on reverse side):

NAME _____

ADDRESS _____

CITY/STATE/ZIP _____

FROM: _____

FOOD FIRST PUBLICATIONS CATALOGS

Please send a Publications Catalog to:

NAME _____

ADDRESS _____

CITY/STATE/ZIP _____

NAME _____

ADDRESS _____

CITY/STATE/ZIP _____

NAME _____

ADDRESS _____

CITY/STATE/ZIP _____

FOOD FIRST GIFT MEMBERSHIPS

❑ Enclosed is my tax-deductible contribution of:

❑ $30   ❑ $50   ❑ $100   ❑ $500   ❑ $1,000

Please send a Food First membership to:

NAME _____

ADDRESS _____

CITY/STATE/ZIP _____

FROM: _____

JOINING FOOD FIRST

❒ I want to join Food First and receive a 20% discount
on this and all subsequent orders. Enclosed
is my tax-deductible contribution of:

❒ $100   ❒ $50   ❒ $30

NAME _____

ADDRESS _____

CITY/STATE/ZIP _____

DAYTIME PHONE (_____) _____

E-MAIL _____

ORDERING FOOD FIRST MATERIALS

ITEM DESCRIPTION	QTY	UNIT COST	TOTAL

PAYMENT METHOD:

❒ CHECK

❒ MONEY ORDER

❒ MASTERCARD

❒ VISA

MEMBER DISCOUNT, 20% $ _____

CA RESIDENTS SALES TAX 8.25% $ _____

SUBTOTAL $ _____

POSTAGE: 15%   UPS: 20%   ($2 MIN.) $ _____

MEMBERSHIP(S) $ _____

ADDITIONAL CONTRIBUTION $ _____

TOTAL ENCLOSED $ _____

NAME ON CARD _____

CARD NUMBER _____ EXP. DATE _____

SIGNATURE _____

MAKE CHECK OR MONEY ORDER PAYABLE TO:
Food First, 398 - 60th Street, Oakland, CA 94618